Contents

Please check the opening times of the houses with the Tourist Information Centre.

The Birth

William Shakespeare was born on 23 April 1564, six years after Elizabeth I became Queen. The date coincides with the Feast of St George, the patron saint of England – so two great symbols of English culture and nationalism are traditionally celebrated on the same day.

His baptism is recorded in the register of Holy Trinity Church in 1564: 'April 26: Gulielmus filius Johannes Shakespere'.

He was born in the upstairs bedroom at Henley Street, and was one of eight children. Mary Arden, his mother, had been brought up in the countryside in Wilmcote, with her seven sisters; her father, Robert Arden, was a successful farmer and landowner.

John Shakespeare, William's father, came from Snitterfield, a village some miles away from Stratford, and was a successful tradesman.

All the world's a stage,
And all the men and women merely players:
They have their exits and their entrances;
And one man in his time plays many parts,
His acts being seven ages. At first the infant,
Mewling and puking in the nurse's arms.
As You Like It, Act 2, Scene 7.
Jaques speaking.

He worked with soft leather, making belts, purses, aprons and gloves, and he also sold wool and barley. It is not surprising that he did well – the most important of England's products during the 16th century were woollen cloth and barley. The barley was used to make beer and ale – and, as this was Stratford's principal industry, John did very well. John Shakespeare was a respected man who took an active part in the civic life of the town. In 1568 he was made bailiff, a position corresponding to mayor.

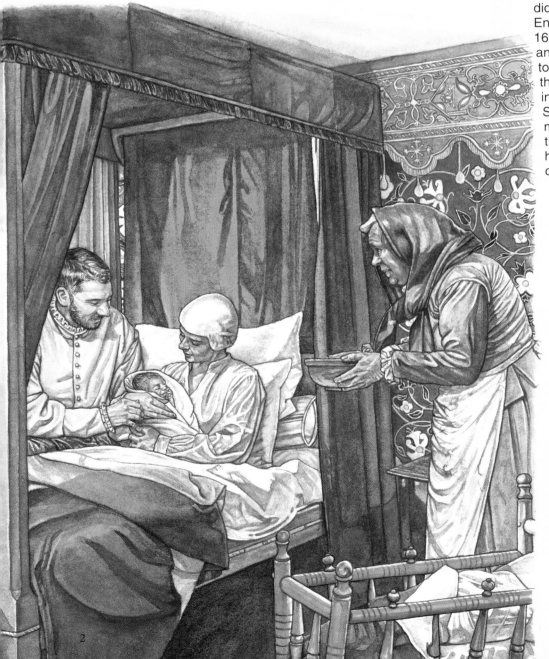

This is the room in Henley Street where, tradition claims, William Shakespeare was born. Make sure that on your visit, you ask to see the leaded lights of the old window in the room. Over the years a number of distinguished visitors have scratched their names on to the glass. No, you can't add yours to the list – the practice has since been stopped!

The Schoolboy

William Shakespeare went to the local Grammar School in Stratford-upon-Avon. It was then called the King's New School (now changed to King Edward VI Grammar School). It is believed that the schoolroom was on the first floor.

William didn't go on to university and, judging from what he says about schools in his plays, he doesn't seem to have had a very happy time! 'Love goes towards love, as schoolboys from their books,' sighs Romeo beneath Juliet's window.

Even though the great religious houses were closed down during the Reformation, the number of people who could read grew during the mid-16th century.

William's education was typically Tudor. The 'grammar' schools were the most common form of education, and they were free. He would have been taught Latin by a well-paid Oxford graduate. Apparently he didn't learn very much because his friend and admirer, Ben Jonson, said he had 'small Latin and less Greek'. However, he would have read Cato, Aesop, Virgil and Horace.

He would also have learnt the Catechism in English and Latin. The Bible, the Book of Common Prayer and the Homilies (sermons published in 1547 and 1563) would have guided his thoughts. The Bible had by then been translated into English by the two great protestants William Tyndale and Miles Coverdale. It presented an English version of Christianity which to the puritan mind laid down the law on the way life should be lived. They believed everything that was written in it and, as far as they were concerned, it needed no interpretation – anyone could read and understand it. This meant that the sense of mystery, captured by the use of allegory and metaphor in the Bible, was lost.

Although Shakespeare was brought up with these orthodox protestant teachings, and although he conformed outwardly, he managed to remain open-minded and inwardly a free-thinker. The Bible is a constant source of inspiration to him, yet his plays lack the rigidity of dogma.

... the whining school-boy, with his satchel,
And shining morning face, creeping like snail
Unwillingly to school.
As You Like It, Act 2, Scene 7.
Jaques speaking.

An Elizabethan Schoolday
The schoolday was tough for a young boy. An early start – 6 a.m. in the summer and 7 a.m. in the winter. A break for lunch at 11 a.m. and then back again at 1 p.m. for another 4 hours with only a 15-minute rest. Discipline would have been strict and the use of the birch was not uncommon.

3

Growing Up

Stratford-upon-Avon was a flourishing market town with about 300 – 400 houses, and at the time that Shakespeare lived had been granted a Royal Charter.

It wasn't a busy place, but on fair days farmers, weavers, dyers, carpenters and shoemakers would bring their goods into the town to sell to locals and passers-by. Travellers who were on their way to Birmingham, clothmaking Coventry (famous for its caps), and the great ports of London and Bristol would stop at the Bear or Swan for a glass of famous Stratford beer or ale. They would arrive hungry and thirsty, but, once rested, they would join the crowds exchanging news, and buy and sell merchandise in the market-place.

The Tudors had changed the old moral order created by the Catholic Church. William lived in a society where people were told that Queen Elizabeth I was God's deputy on earth, and rebellion against the crown was considered a sin against God. Imprisonment, torture or execution were punishments for not going along with these beliefs. People had by law to go to church on Sunday, and were fined if they didn't.

Later, plays were used by some to teach people that rebellion was evil and to spread ideas that would encourage the nation to accept royal authority as legitimate. Others, however, who disagreed with these ideas, used the theatre to undermine authority in the hope that they could change people's ideas. Theatres were therefore accused of being places where sinful people, who were against the state, could gather.

Anyone who challenged the existing order would have been called subversive and Shakespeare knew this. However, he showed how rulers would make and keep themselves great and powerful and at the same time he managed to expose their characters, their fears, and their strengths and weaknesses.

Even though Henry VIII had broken with Rome some time ago, Catholics and Protestants continued to quarrel. There were still English nobles who wanted to remove Elizabeth and replace her with the Catholic Queen of Scotland, Mary. During this time the hatred of everything Catholic grew, and it is thought that William's father suffered financially because he disagreed about the break with Rome. This may not be the true cause – there was a general economic recession and he may also have spent too much time on his duties as bailiff.

Theatre is an ancient art; in England, in the middle ages, when most people couldn't read or write, monks would act out scenes from the Bible with a storyteller explaining what was happening. After a while the actors would make up their own words. You can imagine the plays taking place in the churches underneath the wonderful stained-glass windows and sculptures. The plays became so popular that they eventually moved outside the churches.

In Elizabethan times, England was not known as Merry England for nothing! Marriage, a birth, a wake or one of the different festivals such as Candlemas, Shrove Tuesday, Hocktide, May Day, Whitsuntide, Midsummer Eve, Harvest, Hallowe'en and the twelve days of the Christmas season ending in Twelfth Night demanded some form of celebration. There were sports and feast days, morris dances, sword dances, wassailings, mock ceremonies of summer kings and queens, lords of misrule, mummings, pageants and masques.

Acting was part of local village culture, and this did not just mean studying a part, but also allowed the player to become a vessel through which something else could be expressed. The celebrations and rituals gave people a release from the controls and conventions of everyday life, where the distinctions between life and art, and the stage and life, could merge and disappear.

Amateur actors from the surrounding villages, in search of an audience, would come to town on market-day, and the theme of the amateur actor and his good-natured yet clumsy performances is used in Shakespeare's plays.

In the 16th century plays were performed in the courtyards of inns. The actors would put up a temporary stage opposite the main entrance and the audience could then sit around the three sides of the stage. If you had enough money you would be able to pay the innkeeper for the privilege of sitting in a balcony overlooking the courtyard.

As a young boy, and later as a young man, William would help his father with his work. In those days glovers had a privileged position. Their trade was protected against foreign competition by an Act of Parliament. On market-day they would stand underneath the clock at the Market Cross, the most important place in the town. While he was there William would have had plenty of opportunity to see plays and meet players from the many bands of professional players who travelled around the country, perhaps escaping from London when there was an outbreak of the plague.

All this must have been a wonderful experience for a small boy whose imagination would have been stirred by what he saw and heard. The village celebrations; strange tales told by sailors coming back from foreign lands; arguments about the struggle for the freedom of speech. Last but not least, William would have been able to watch play after play, an on-going delight for any small child, especially one with his imagination.

St George and the Dragon was a well-known play which was performed at Christmas.

5

Marriage

In spite of a busy life William still found time for romance. He married Anne Hathaway in November 1582. Anne was the daughter of Richard Hathaway, a farmer who lived at Shottery, a mile outside Stratford-upon-Avon. When they married, William probably took Anne to live with him at his father's house in Henley Street; it was not unusual for two families to live together.

William was only eighteen and a half, Anne was eight years older. The marriage was rushed as Anne was three months' pregnant; Susanna was born in May 1583. It was most unusual for a man of William's age to get married, and as she was so much older than him, it would be nice to know whether they married because they fell in love, or because Anne was carrying his child. No one will ever really know the truth, and sadly we do not even know if he ever composed any ballads for her.

It must have been a relief for the Hathaways to see their daughter safely married – and not only because she was pregnant. It is unlikely that Anne could read or write and in a world made for men she would have found it difficult to earn a living because women were excluded from public life.

Unmarried women had traditionally gone into the church, but after the English Reformation, when Henry VIII closed the monasteries and took their wealth, many women took to the road. The most an unmarried woman could hope for was to be a servant in someone else's house, or to be kept by her own family.

Shakespeare was aware of the difficulties women faced and in many of his plays he shows how they are ill-treated, abused and bartered to the highest bidder. He also shows them dressing up as men in order to be treated on an equal basis. However, in the tragedies he describes men as being dominated and destroyed by women.

If you take the footpaths across the fields to reach Anne's house you will be able to enjoy the same scenes that surrounded the courting couple. Make sure that when you visit Anne Hathaway's cottage you imagine Anne and William in front of the fire sitting on the settle.

Let me not to the marriage of true minds
Admit impediments. Love is not love
Which alters when it alteration finds,
Or bends with the remover to remove:
O, no! it is an ever-fixed mark,
That looks on tempests
 and is never shaken;
It is the star to every wandering bark,
Whose worth's unknown,
 although his height be taken.
Love's not Time's fool,
 though rosy lips and cheeks
Within his bending sickle's
 compass come;
Love alters not with his brief
 hours and weeks,
But bears it out even to the edge of doom.
If this be error, and upon me prov'd,
I never writ, nor no man ever lov'd.
Sonnets,116.

Family Life

We don't know what Shakespeare did before he went to London. Some say he stayed in Stratford, led a domestic life and helped his father to run the family business. Some say he worked in a lawyer's office, others say he was a country schoolmaster or that he worked in a great household or as a soldier in the Low Countries. Whatever he did it is something of a mystery, and it is impossible to say whether the characters in his plays are speaking from Shakespeare's own experiences or from his imagination.

Family life did not seem to dampen William's spirits, and gossip, that appears to have survived to this day, reports (and this may not be true!) that he was friends with a rowdy set of young men who would steal deer from Sir Thomas Lucy's park at Charlecote. Sir Thomas even threatened to prosecute William. However, William's reply to the threat was a mischievous note which he tied on to the park gates:

> A parliament member,
>   a justice of peace
> At home a poor scarecrow,
>   in London an asse
> If Lucy is Lowsie as some
>   folk miscall it
> Sing Lowsie Lucy whatever
>   befall it.

The Shakespeare fortunes were at a low ebb, and with all the extra little mouths to feed, the Henley Street house must have felt quite crowded. William and Anne had three children; Susanna was born six months after their marriage. Two years later, in 1585, the twins were born – a boy, Hamnet, and a girl, Judith. In spite of his love for his family, it must have been quite frustrating for a man with his creativity and intelligence to live under these circumstances. It was only in London that a man with his talents could get ahead and make a career for himself.

No: as a walled town is more worthier than a village,
so is the forehead of a married man more honourable than the bare brow of a bachelor.
As You Like It, Act 3, Scene 3. Touchstone speaking.

It was probably in 1587 that he went to London. Five companies of actors visited Stratford that year; some people say that he made friends with a number of actors and either went off with them to London or got in touch with them when he arrived in the city. With the family business in difficulties he may not have had enough money for a horse. He would have walked south via Banbury or Oxford; it would have taken him at least 4 days to reach London and that would be going at a brisk 25 miles a day.

Shakespeare's life in London can be traced from 1592 onwards, first as an actor, then as a reviser and writer of plays.

The Struggle to Succeed

When Shakespeare arrived in London it was a most exciting time. Mary Queen of Scots had just been executed, Phillip II of Spain was building up the Armada and London was preparing for the invasion. Drake was the terror of the Spanish Main, Raleigh was at Court and contemporaries included Marlowe, Bacon, Spenser and Jonson.

Although puritanical dislike of the theatre was slowly growing into the hostility which, just over half a century later, overwhelmed English drama completely, the theatres were still very popular. The puritans had already started harassing actors to try and stop them from performing. The theatre was the only place where people could go and hear honest comments about life, and audiences must have gone with a sense of mischief, keen to spot hidden meanings.

Coaches were not yet common in Elizabethan England and people who disliked walking would get around the city on horseback. Those arriving at the theatre would need someone to mind their horses and a popular story about Shakespeare was that he soon set himself up in a small business minding horses. Acquiring a reputation for honesty, people soon asked for him. In no time at all, he had more business than he could cope with, and he hired a number of young boys whom he would send on his behalf. They would present themselves and say, 'I am Shakespeare's boy, Sir.'

The standard of living was low and a skilled workman in the City of London would have earned 10d. (old pence) to 14d. a day and it cost 1d. to go to the theatre. Shakespeare's first job in the theatre may have been that of a prompter's attendant. Traditionally, all new members of a theatre company would have to take this job, which simply meant that he

would call the actors when they were to make an appearance on stage.

Shakespeare and his fellow players were lucky enough to be able to win the patronage of Lord Hunsdon, the Lord Chamberlain, and his company came to be called the Lord Chamberlain's Men. The company was made up of about a dozen actors. The actors would double and treble their roles so that in a single play they could introduce 20 or 30 characters. Very little time was given to group rehearsals and actors were only given the words of their own parts. The most important scenes were played between two and three actors or one character would dominate a crowded stage. Shakespeare wrote his plays with the skills of his actors in mind.

When Shakespeare became a professional actor he liked living near his work but his success in London did not mean he left his family for good; he would often return home to Stratford and the pleasures of family life.

Speak the speech, I pray you,
*   as I pronounced it to you,*
*   trippingly on the tongue;*
*   but if you mouth it,*
*   as many of your players do,*
*   I had as lief the town-crier spoke*
*   my lines.*
Nor do not saw the air too much
*   with your hand,*
*   thus; but use all gently:*
Hamlet, Act 3, Scene 2.
Hamlet speaking.

Mary Arden's House at Wilmcote

William Shakespeare's mother was brought up in this lovely farmhouse. Most of the building is 16th-century and only minor changes have been made to it over the years. There is also a marvellous sprawl of old barns belonging to the farmhouse and to the Glebe Farm buildings nearby. They are filled with a very interesting exhibition of old farm implements, rural life exhibits and crafts.

By looking at the house you can tell that the Ardens were wealthier than the Hathaways. Firstly the timbers of the house are closer together – more timbers meant they could afford the wood. Secondly, they had a dovecote or pigeon house with 657 nesting holes – the keeping of pigeons was usually restricted to the Lord of the Manor.

The kitchen
The kitchen has a paved stone floor, which originally would have been made of earth and covered with layers of loose rushes and sweet smelling herbs. The floor covering would stay there until the end of May when spring cleaning would begin. Although the windows are now made of small panes of leaded glass, the windows then were made of cowhorn; this allowed the light to come in but anyone inside the house couldn't see out.

About fifteen people would have lived in this house so you can imagine how much they ate. Potatoes hadn't yet arrived in England and bread and biscuits were made in the bake-oven that used to be alongside the open fireplace. Carcases and birds were cooked on the spit. Afterwards the fat would be used for making candles.

The Great Hall
The Great Hall was the main meeting place in the house. Originally there wasn't a ceiling in the centre part of the house and the two sleeping lofts were reached by climbing up ladders.

The settle, which is probably 17th-century, is also known as a spooning settle. It is said that once a man started courting he would be given a piece of wood and expected to carve it while talking to his beloved. On the wedding day he would give the spoon to his bride. The father of the house would sit in the chair opposite the settle and keep a watchful eye on the couple.

The **servants' room** leads off from the hall and the **dairy** is on your left. This is the coolest room in the house and is filled with old milk pails and butter and cheese-making utensils.

Where the bee sucks, there suck I
In a cowslip's bell I lie;
There I couch when owls do cry.
On the bat's back I do fly
After summer merrily:
Merrily, merrily shall I live now
Under the blossom that hangs
    on the bough.
The Tempest, Act 5, Scene 1.
Ariel singing.

Upstairs
Look at the roof and you will see how trees have been roughly shaped and used for the main beams, then look at how they have been jointed and fastened together with wooden pegs.

Stratford-upon-Avon

Make your visit to Stratford-upon-Avon a memorable and enriching experience by exploring the places shown on this map. The properties run by the Shakespeare Birthplace Trust are staffed by well-informed guides who are willing to tell you everything you need to know about Shakespeare's life, the furniture and the various exhibitions.

① SHAKESPEARE CENTRE *

This centre was built by the Shakespeare Birthplace Trust to celebrate the 400th anniversary of Shakespeare's birth. There are always fascinating exhibitions in the hall.

② SHAKESPEARE'S BIRTHPLACE *

Shakespeare was born in this half-timbered house in Henley Street. Make sure you see the room in which tradition claims he was born.

③ NASH'S HOUSE *

Thomas Nash was the first husband of Shakespeare's granddaughter, Elizabeth Hall. In the house you will find an interesting collection of furniture, local archaeological and historical material. When Thomas Nash died, Elizabeth later married Sir John Barnard of Abingdon. She had no children from either of her two marriages and she died in 1670.

④ THE FOUNDATIONS OF NEW PLACE *

Here are the foundations of the house to which Shakespeare retired. It had been built in 1483 by Hugh Clopton. This was a fine timber-framed house but, unlike most of the houses of its day, the gaps between the wooden struts were not filled with wattle and daub (plastered basketwork) but with good red bricks. It is thought that it was one of the first houses in Stratford to be built of bricks. New Place was destroyed by the

Reverend Francis Gastrell, who in 1756 chopped down the mulberry tree that Shakespeare had planted in the Great Garden, and went on to pull the house down in 1759. Apparently, he couldn't bear the constant stream of sightseers wanting to look at this famous house. Do go to the back of Nash's House, where there is a replica of an Elizabethan Knot Garden. You will also be able to walk around Shakespeare's Great Garden, which contained his orchard and his kitchen garden.

⑤ KING EDWARD VI GRAMMAR SCHOOL

Shakespeare went to this Grammar School. The school was founded in the 13th century and the first schoolmaster recorded was in 1401. The school-house was built in 1426 and refounded by Edward VI in 1553.

denotes Shakespeare Birthplace Trust property

3. Nash's House

6. Hall's Croft

7. Holy Trinity Church

9. Anne Hathaway's Cottage, Shottery

10. Mary Arden's House, Wilmcote

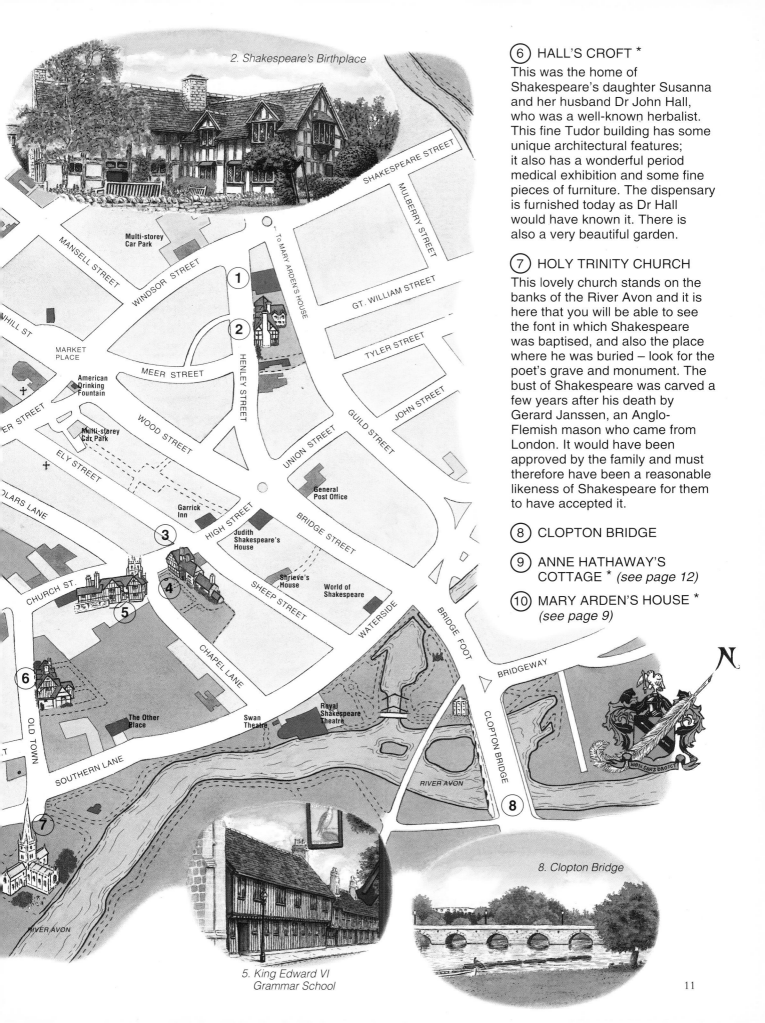

2. Shakespeare's Birthplace

5. King Edward VI Grammar School

8. Clopton Bridge

6 HALL'S CROFT *

This was the home of Shakespeare's daughter Susanna and her husband Dr John Hall, who was a well-known herbalist. This fine Tudor building has some unique architectural features; it also has a wonderful period medical exhibition and some fine pieces of furniture. The dispensary is furnished today as Dr Hall would have known it. There is also a very beautiful garden.

7 HOLY TRINITY CHURCH

This lovely church stands on the banks of the River Avon and it is here that you will be able to see the font in which Shakespeare was baptised, and also the place where he was buried – look for the poet's grave and monument. The bust of Shakespeare was carved a few years after his death by Gerard Janssen, an Anglo-Flemish mason who came from London. It would have been approved by the family and must therefore have been a reasonable likeness of Shakespeare for them to have accepted it.

8 CLOPTON BRIDGE

9 ANNE HATHAWAY'S COTTAGE * (see page 12)

10 MARY ARDEN'S HOUSE * (see page 9)

Anne Hathaway's Cottage at Shottery

This was the home of Shakespeare's wife, Anne. She was born here in 1556, and lived here until she married William in 1582. This picturesque thatched cottage with its half-timbered white-washed walls represents for many people the essence of domestic architecture created in Tudor England. It is in fact pre-Tudor in its earliest form. Some of the wood used for the building dates from 1462 and the house includes an early form of timber construction known as crucks. It is now surrounded by a beautiful old-fashioned garden filled with traditional English flowers, herbs, clipped box hedges, shrubs and trees. When William's wife Anne was growing up it would have been a farmyard.

Descendants of the Hathaway family lived here until as recently as 1892. Much of the furniture in the house was used by the family over the years. There are many interesting relics which the guides will tell you about. All you need to do is to ask.

The living room or hall
Have a look at the wide open hearth; most farmhouses in this period would have been built like this. If you look at the back you will be able to see a couple of square recesses. These would have been used as tinder holes. The bacon would have been put in the space behind the latticed door.

The buttery
This was a working room and if you look carefully at the utensils, you'll see that they are used for making butter and salting meat.

The upstairs chamber
This room will give you an idea of the style in which the farmhouse would have been furnished. The furniture did not belong to the Hathaways but includes appropriate examples dating from that period.

The bedroom
This room was the principal bedroom and has in it a wonderful, finely-carved late-Elizabethan joined bed. The mattress couldn't have been too comfortable – it is made of rush supported on cords. The finely decorated needlework sheet is a family heirloom.

Anne's room
Tradition claims that Anne's room is next door. It is a simply furnished room containing a four-poster bed with its original linsey-wool hangings.

The kitchen
You will probably love this room with its low ceiling and small latticed windows. The open fireplace would have been used for cooking. Have a look at the spit, drip pan and other cooking utensils. There is an oven for baking bread at the back.

The room over the kitchen
This would have been used as a store room.

*I know a bank whereon the
 wild thyme blows,
Where oxlips and the nodding
 violet grows
Quite over-canopied with luscious
 woodbine,
With sweet musk-roses,
 and with eglantine:
There sleeps Titania some time
 of the night,
Lull'd in these flowers with
 dances and delight;*
A Midsummer Night's Dream, Act 2, Scene 1.
Oberon speaking.

Success

In 1597 William bought New Place, one of the largest and most beautiful houses in Elizabethan Stratford. He paid for it out of his share of the profits made in the Lord Chamberlain's Company. The house had been built by Hugh Clopton, a Lord Mayor of London – another local boy who had made good, who also improved the guild chapel which is almost opposite New Place and built the fine stone bridge over the River Avon.

The house was opposite his old school and Shakespeare would have walked past it every day as a boy. Little did he then realise what heights he was destined for. Now, from his garden, it was his turn to watch the boys coming and going. How sad it was for him not to see his own son amongst them. Hamnet had died the previous year, aged 11. Shakespeare was then 33, Anne 41, and daughters Susanna 14 and Judith 12.

There is probably no doubt that some of his manuscripts were written at New Place. First produced in rough and called the 'foul papers', they would later have been copied by Shakespeare, or by somebody else. The play would then be licensed for the stage and go into production.

Although literature was England's greatest art form there is nothing to show that Shakespeare was concerned about his plays being printed. He wrote to please theatre audiences who would pay to come and listen to them. Not everybody could read and he didn't write for a reading public. It appears that the company would assert its rights in a play when it had been printed without its agreement, or when it needed some extra money.

Shakespeare's plays may well have been popular with Queen Elizabeth I, who loved music and drama. When James I came to the throne in 1603, he recognised Shakespeare and his company as

the leading group of actors, and from then on they were known as the King's Men.

Shakespeare's father, John, died in 1601, living just long enough to see his son make a great success of his life. However, not everybody was as lucky; of the 2,000 people living in Stratford over 300 were claiming poor relief. The corporation had even warned the alehouse keepers not to increase their misery by selling strong drink.

In 1605 Shakespeare bought the tithes to some land – this was a good investment. In England and Wales the population had increased from 2.2 million in 1525 to 4 million in 1603. With the great increase in births, food prices had risen sharply and there was not enough food. The yeoman farmers who had at least 100 acres of land seemed to be able to survive as they were able to offer employment and produce food which people were willing to buy.

Shakespeare made enough money to build a comfortable life. In 1596, the Shakespeare family were given their coat of arms. The motto chosen was *Non sanz droict* – not without right.

The Family Grows Up

In 1607 Shakespeare's daughter, Susanna, now aged 24, married John Hall and went to live with him at the property now known as Hall's Croft. A year later, Elizabeth, their daughter, was born, in the same year that Shakespeare's mother, Mary, died.

John Hall was a successful doctor and a most interesting man. It is thought that Shakespeare gained most of his knowledge about medicine from him. Shakespeare left New Place to John and Susanna in his will, and they moved there after he died.

Dr Hall was the son of a well-to-do Bedfordshire physician and was brought up in Carlton, about 30 miles from Cambridge. He settled in Stratford around 1600 after completing his MA degree at Queen's College in 1594.

John Hall treated all sorts of diseases and was a great herbalist. He was well known for his remedy for scurvy, a disease caused by the Elizabethan diet which, although rich in salted meat and fish, was deficient in fresh fruit and vegetables. His remedy was rich in vitamin C and contained watercress, brooklime, scurvy grass and various other roots and herbs. The mixture was then boiled in beer and flavoured with sugar, cinnamon and juniper berries.

Shakespeare's granddaughter, Elizabeth, married Thomas Nash and lived in the house next door to New Place. When Thomas died she married Sir John Barnard of Abingdon. She had no children from either of her two marriages and she died in 1670.

Shakespeare's other daughter, Judith, married Thomas Quiney in 1616. Not much is known about him; some say he was a drunk. They had three sons, but all died without leaving any children.

My noble father,
I do perceive here a divided duty;
To you I am bound for life and education;
My life and education both do learn me
How to respect you;
*   you are the lord of duty,*
I am hitherto your daughter:
*   but here's my husband;*
And so much duty as my mother show'd
To you, preferring you before her father,
So much I challenge that I may profess
Due to the Moor, my lord.
Othello, Act 1, Scene 3.
Desdemona speaking.

Death

In an age when few men lived past 60, Shakespeare, now nearly 52, made his will. It was completed on 25 March 1616. Almost exactly a month later, tradition claims, after spending an enjoyable evening with his friends Michael Drayton and Ben Jonson, Shakespeare fell ill with a temperature. He did not recover and died on 23 April 1616 – the same day as his birth. He was exactly 52 years old. Two days later, his funeral service took place in Holy Trinity Church, where he had been christened.

On his grave you will find this written:

> Good friend, for Jesus'
>   sake forbeare
> To digg the dust enclosed
>   heare;
> Bleste be yee man yt spares
>   these stones
> And curst be he yt moves
>   my bones.

Inside the church is a bust of Shakespeare. The words underneath him read:

> Stay passenger, why goest thou
>   by so fast?
> Read if thou canst whom
>   envious death hath placed
> Within this monument,
> Shakespeare, with whom
> Quick nature dide: whose name
>   doth deck this tomb
> Far more than cost:
>   sith all that he has writ
> Leaves living art but page
>   to serve his wit.

His burial is recorded in the register as follows:

'April 25 Will.
Shakespeare gent.'

To-morrow, and to-morrow,
    and to-morrow,
Creeps in this petty pace from day to day,
To the last syllable of recorded time;
And all our yesterdays have lighted fools
The way to dusty death.
    Out, out, brief candle!
Life's but a walking shadow, a poor player
That struts and frets his hour
    upon the stage,
And then is heard no more; it is a tale
Told by an idiot, full of sound and fury,
Signifying nothing.
Macbeth, Act 5, Scene 5. Macbeth speaking.

The Elizabethan Theatre

The theatre that Shakespeare grew up in, acted in and wrote for was very different from the theatre we have today. There was no front curtain separating the audience from the stage and Elizabethan actors had very different ideas on how to create the illusion of reality. Perhaps we would find it difficult to lose ourselves in a play where it was daylight and female parts were written for young male actors and boys.

Stage in an inn yard

Costumes were very important and, as the lives of the rich and the poor were very different, the rich showed off their wealth in silk, linen or woollen clothing. The poor would wear simple clothes of leather or wool.

Apart from an occasional backcloth, very little scenery was used. A potted tree would symbolise a forest, a few plates an inn. The time, the place and the mood were created by the actors. For example:

> *The moon shines bright.*
> *In such a night as this*
> *When the sweet wind*
>   *did gently kiss the trees,*
> *And they did make no noise,*
>   *in such a night...*
> The Merchant of Venice,
> Act 5, Scene 1.
> Lorenzo speaking.

Plays were also produced in private houses, town halls and inn-yards. You may find it interesting that the designs for the first purpose-built theatre used the same ideas as those of the open inn-yard. You may wonder why. Perhaps they were frightened – there was a perpetual risk of the plague. It spread more easily in closed, crowded conditions as it was passed from person to person by fleas living on the rats which thrived in the filthy London streets.

Swan   Globe   Rose   Bear Garden

Swan Theatre as it might have looked

Public theatres were open to the sky and built of wood. They were polygonal or rectangular. The stage, like the inn-yard platforms, jutted out about half way into the auditorium. The audience would stand all around it or pay to sit on stools on the stage. Others who could afford to would sit in the inner galleries built on the inside walls, protected from the rain. There was a curtained recess at the back of the stage (the discovery space). This space could be used to show a separate scene or room, although sight lines make it impossible to believe that whole scenes were ever played there. There was also an upper storey which could be used as a balcony (for example, in Romeo and Juliet's famous scene). Above the first balcony there was another room in which the musicians would sit and play. Over the stage was a canopy which was painted blue and decorated with stars. Underneath the main stage there was a space (the cellarage), which the audience could not see, and on the stage a number of trapdoors.

Shakespeare's company used one of the best theatres in London, and when the lease ran out they pulled it down and rebuilt it on Bankside. Shakespeare had a share in the new theatre, called the Globe, along with William Kemp and other actors. At a performance of *Henry VIII,* on 29 June 1613, a cannon was used to mark the entrance of the King in Act I, Scene IV. A cannon-ball accidentally hit the thatched roof and within a short time the whole building burnt to the ground.

The Globe was rebuilt and the second Globe survived with a tiled roof until 1642. A third Globe – a working replica of the original – was opened on the same site in 1997.

Later, another kind of theatre (hall theatres) was built which attracted a wealthier type of person, and the poor were then excluded from these. The new theatres were smaller and gave the impression that the plays were being performed in a private house. The roof was closed and artificial lighting was used. During the winter Shakespeare's company moved north of the Thames to the Blackfriars theatre, which was a hall theatre.

Shakespearean Theatre Today

Today, if we are to be cast upon a desert island, Shakespeare and the Bible are the two books the BBC will allow us to have. This in itself says something about Shakespeare and the enduring quality of his plays.

Of course, many things have changed since the 16th century. Women now act, and actors are no longer thought of as ruffians; in fact, an actor (Ronald Reagan) has even become President of the United States of America. The theatre has now become respectable and its function goes beyond mere entertainment – so much so that we use public money to support it and, like the National Health Service, we think it is important for the nation's health.

Many of the plays have now been performed in styles very different from their original settings. This has given the characters life of their own, and given directors the freedom to put the plays into any period and language they want. For example, *Julius Caesar*, as an example of totalitarianism, can be played in togas, jackboots or dinner jackets; *A Midsummer Night's Dream* in Doc Martens or ballet pumps. The human emotions and themes remain the same, whatever the period or the dress. If authors are judged on their ability to invest their characters with so much energy that they can live a life of their own, then Shakespeare's works have passed this test.

When we think about the theatre we also have to think about the type of audience watching the play and the reaction they have to the text and the way in which the director and actors interpret the text. In any play, the text is the bare minimum and playwrights can't provide detailed instructions on rhythm, stress, tempo and inflexion. They can provide punctuation, but much of the punctuation in Shakespeare's works has been changed by various editors, and also by different companies in their search for new meaning. There are traditional ways of speaking Shakespeare and the Royal Shakespeare Company are known for their more classical interpretations. Other companies are more experimental, using Shakespeare as the basis for the dramatic action and saying the words differently or in a modern style. Like a piece of music, the text is the musical score where the performance carries the interpretation.

Audiences have also changed. What is acceptable in the way of theatre today would have been unacceptable in Shakespeare's time. When people watch a Shakespearean play today what do they want? Do they go to the theatre for an opportunity to

The Gower Memorial in Bancroft Gardens

inspect an archaeological reconstruction, another copy of the original that has perhaps outlived its purpose? Or for something that confirms present-day values, such as a *Taming of the Shrew* presented as a feminist statement on male brutality, rather than as an account of Elizabethan values? Or do they go looking for a reinterpretation, where the play is treated as virgin land about to be explored, not something that is solid and unmovable?

Enjoying Shakespeare in performance brings out the many layers of meaning in the plays in a way that words on the page cannot. The search for meaning is one of the reasons why Shakespearean theatre has remained popular to this day.

Shakespeare wrote his plays to be performed, not to be read. He knew that the actors had a special role to play in interpreting the archetypal characters, who help us to imagine and understand their and our own experiences and the world around.

The first memorial theatre was opened on Shakespeare's birthday in 1879. Charles Edward Flower, head of the local brewing company, gave the site and most of the £20,000 which it cost to build. A fire burnt most of it down in 1926 and a new theatre, designed by Elizabeth Scott, was built in 1932. It seats 1500 people and is one of the most modern and well-equipped theatres in the world. The new Swan Theatre, in the style of an Elizabethan playhouse, was constructed within the remains of the old building and was opened in 1986.

No visit to Stratford-upon-Avon is complete without a visit to the home of the Royal Shakespeare Company. The theatre is a living memorial to the great man and many great British actors and actresses have performed on its boards. During their stay, visitors can see more than one play, as the company selects a number of plays which are performed 'in repertory'.

Royal Shakespeare Theatre

Swan Theatre

Brush up your Shakespeare – Test Yourself

Here are some well-known lines that Shakespeare wrote – see if you can guess the play they come from. If so, see if you can remember who said it and to whom they said it. The correct answers are at the bottom of the page. Enjoy yourself!

1. So wise, so young, they say do never live long.

2. Something is rotten in the state of Denmark.

3. The moon, methinks, looks with a watery eye;

4. The fault, dear Brutus, is not in our stars
But in ourselves, that we are underlings.

5. The evil that men do lives after them,
The good is oft interred with their bones;

6. Tell me, where is fancy bred
Or in the heart or in the head?

7. To sleep: perchance to dream! Ay there's the rub,
For in that sleep of death what dreams may come,
When we have shuffled off this mortal coil,
Must give us pause.

8. A horse! A horse! My kingdom for a horse!

9. Assume a virtue if you have it not.

10. Comparisons are odorous:

11. Double, double toil and trouble;

12. Every subject's duty is the King's; but every subject's soul is his own.

13. Now is the Winter of our discontent Made glorious Summer by this son of York.

14. Parting is such sweet sorrow...

15. Oh, beware, my lord, of jealousy;
It is the green-eyed monster, which doth mock
The meat it feeds on.

16. Neither a borrower nor a lender be:

17. It is a wise father that knows his own child...

18. The quality of mercy is not strained;

19. To be, or not to be: that is the question:

20. Where the bee sucks, there suck I:

21. When beggars die, there are no comets seen;

22. Lovers and madmen have such seething brains,
Such shaping fantasies that apprehend
More than cool reason ever comprehends.

Answers

1. The tragedy of King Richard III – Act 3, Scene 1. Gloucester speaking.
2. Hamlet, Prince of Denmark – Act 1, Scene 4. Marcellus speaking.
3. A Midsummer Night's Dream – Act 3, Scene 1. Titania speaking.
4. Julius Caesar – Act 1, Scene 2. Cassius speaking.
5. Julius Caesar – Act 3, Scene 2. Antony speaking.
6. The Merchant of Venice – Act 3, Scene 2. Song.
7. Hamlet, Prince of Denmark – Act 3, Scene 1. Hamlet speaking.
8. The Tragedy of King Richard III – Act 5, Scene 4. Richard III speaking.
9. Hamlet, Prince of Denmark – Act 3, Scene 4. Hamlet speaking.
10. Much Ado about Nothing – Act 3, Scene 5. Dogberry speaking.
11. Macbeth – Act 4, Scene 1. The Three Witches speaking.
12. The Life of King Henry V – Act 4, Scene 1. The King speaking.
13. The Tragedy of King Richard III – Act 1, Scene 1. Gloucester speaking.
14. Romeo and Juliet – Act 2, Scene 2. Juliet speaking.
15. Othello, The Moor of Venice – Act 3, Scene 3. Iago speaking.
16. Hamlet, Prince of Denmark – Act 1, Scene 3. Polonius speaking.
17. The Merchant of Venice – Act 2, Scene 2. Launcelot speaking.
18. The Merchant of Venice – Act 4, Scene 1. Portia speaking.
19. Hamlet, Prince of Denmark – Act 3, Scene 1. Hamlet speaking.
20. The Tempest – Act 5, Scene 1. Ariel singing.
21. Julius Caesar – Act 2, Scene 2. Calpurnia speaking.
22. A Midsummer Night's Dream – Act 5, Scene 1. Theseus speaking.

HOW TO
SURVIVE
ANYTHING

CENTENNIAL BOOKS

BE PREPARED FOR ANY SITUATION

APOCALYPSE • BLIZZARD • CHEMICAL WARFARE • CYBERTHREAT
FIRE • FLOOD • HOME INVASION • HURRICANE • MASS SHOOTING • NUCLEAR BLAST
PANDEMIC • PLANE CRASH • SHARK ATTACK • TERRORISM • TORNADO

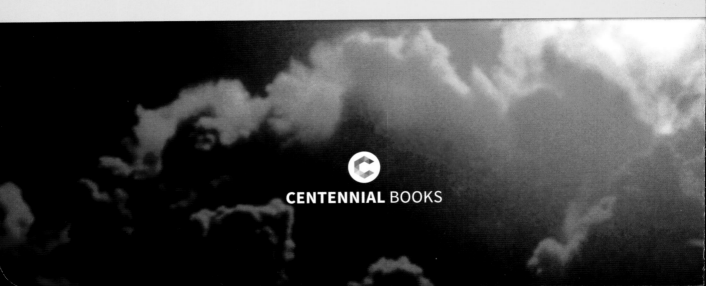

CENTENNIAL BOOKS

HOW TO
SURVIVE
ANYTHING

MICHAEL FLEEMAN

CONTENTS

INTRODUCTION

It looked like an isolated outbreak in a Chinese city in December 2019, but the coronavirus had other ideas. With breakneck speed, it spread to South Korea, Japan, Italy, Germany, France, then to the United States. Movie theaters were closed, restaurants and bars shut down, cruise ships quarantined, planes grounded, factories idled. The interruption in manufacturing supply chains disrupted commerce around the world and sent the markets reeling. Tens of thousands of people died, yet a few months in to the pandemic, nobody could say when it would all stop.

Whether caused by man, nature or technology, disasters seem to come out of nowhere. But while a fact of life, the effects—injury, heartbreak and death—are far from inevitable. While science, political will and money all are vital tools, the best weapon against disasters of any kind is knowledge. And survival depends as much on what you do now as how you act in the moment.

In the pages of this book you'll find practical steps that you can take right now to protect yourself and your family and get peace of mind, plus tips for riding out those storms, attacks, accidents and even doomsday scenarios. This advice is brought to life with first-person accounts from people who stared down disaster and lived to talk about it, like the newspaper reporter who escaped unscathed, if only barely, from Hurricane Irma; the Texas man who floated to safety during flooding in an aluminum fishing boat; the couple who dodged the flames of a Northern California wildfire in a swimming pool; the 10-year-old girl who fended off an alligator by sticking her fingers up its nose; and the airline passenger who relied on a few prayers to keep calm when the roof of the plane ripped off mid-flight.

Even the smallest of actions—like sketching out escape plans and having vital documents like birth certificates and Social Security cards in easy-to-find folders—can make the difference between life and death, helping you to save precious time and get out on a moment's notice before that hurricane, tornado, earthquake or volcanic eruption hits your area.

Make sure your property is disaster-ready: Bolt down those propane tanks in hurricane

and tornado country; install smoke alarms. And always have a radio with fresh batteries (or one that is crank-operated) to get the latest on official announcements, which should never be ignored.

Then stay calm—and rely on your knowledge and preparation. Know in advance that those harmless-looking puddles left after floods and storms could actually be deeper than they appear, hiding sharp objects, or even be electrified from downed power lines. Remember that you likely have more time than you think for help to arrive while you're trapped in your car during a blizzard or even under avalanche snows.

Panic tends to be your biggest enemy, especially in human-caused tragedies, when awareness of your surroundings—sensing danger before it strikes, finding hiding places and exit routes—may protect you during mass shootings, bombings and car-rammings.

So does making the right decision at the right time. Sometimes, fight is better than flight. You'll have nothing to lose—even if that foe is not another human. To show who's boss of the waters, give that shark a bonk on the nose if it won't leave you alone, or make a ruckus to scare off that alligator.

As for the deadliest animal of all—the disease-carrying mosquito—a simple can of insect repellent can do wonders. If all else fails, be sure to know basic first aid, like the use of a tourniquet, and brush up on survival techniques for enduring the heat of a desert or the cold of the mountains. Stay awake during the most dangerous times of air travel, just after takeoff and just before landing, so you'll be ready to act; stay on that sinking ship as long as possible as help may be closer than you think; try to sit facing backward on a train to mitigate the effects of a fast stop; and always, always, always wear your seat belt in the car.

Even in the worst of the worse cases, like the first seconds of a nuclear blast or atomic meltdown, you have options, if you prepare properly and follow basic steps. And surviving a global pandemic like the coronavirus can be as simple as regularly washing your hands with soap and water.

So get your "go-bag" ready. It's not a question of if disaster will strike, but when.
                                                —*Michael Fleeman*

7

CHAPTER 01

NATURE STRIKES BACK

> Mother Nature has been in a foul mood. A recent string of natural disasters has left a path of destruction, injury and death from the Caribbean to California's wine country. Get your household ready and sharpen your survival skills for the next hurricane, tornado, flood, volcano, wildfire, tsunami, earthquake, avalanche, lightning strike and more.

WATER WORLD
New Orleans is still rebuilding from 2005's Hurricane Katrina that burst levees and left much of the city underwater.

HOW TO SURVIVE A

HURRICANE

THE EYES HAVE IT: THESE STORMS ARE GETTING BIGGER AND STRONGER

In a 2019 Weather Company/Morning Consult survey, 74 percent of Americans said they think weather events are getting more severe due to climate change. Exhibit A: the 2019 Atlantic hurricane season, which was notable for two destructive trends. The first: ultra-intense hurricanes like the Category 5 Hurricane Dorian (some experts say it was worth creating a Category 6 rating for). The second: There were also a number of extremely slow-moving storms. They weren't as dramatic, but had catastrophic consequences: They linger over a region for days, bringing heavy rain and dangerous flooding and causing billions in widespread damage.

STAY INDOORS

You know that thing TV weather guys do during a hurricane? Don't do that. Going outside and leaning into the wind when the gusts hit 100 mph-plus and thick tree limbs and metal stop signs start flying is a recipe for disaster. As with most catastrophes, the best response begins long before the first gust of wind. And remember, hurricanes have more than one way to kill. As FEMA points out in its survival tips: "Hurricanes cause deaths and injuries primarily from drowning, wind and wind-borne debris."

LONG-TERM PREP

Ready your escape plan, including getaway road routes and meet-up plans for the family. Compile birth certificates, insurance policies and Social Security cards into easy-to-find folders, and have all your medications in one place. Make a "go-bag" (see page 172 for details). Get potential killer projectiles like outdoor furniture and propane tanks bolted down, and make sure the sewer backflow valves are working.

SHORT-TERM PREP

When it looks like your area might be hit, board up windows and build sandbag barriers around areas prone to flooding. Even minor flooding can cause extensive damage. Keep yourself glued to local news and National Weather Service alerts, taking note of the location of the closest shelters and potential road closures. And don't forget to fuel up your car. If evacuations are ordered, those gasoline lines could be long. Also, make sure your cellphone is fully charged.

GET OUT

There's nothing to prove; it's better to pack up and run away from the danger. But if you wait too long or the storm gets too intense too fast and you find yourself outside, head for high ground and steer clear of flooded streets. You don't know what sharp objects may be hidden under the water. And by all means, don't drive through water, even if it looks shallow. That 6-inch puddle is enough to stall out your car—and can become feet deep very quickly.

AVOID WINDOWS

If you're at home or in an office, close the drapes, keep away from windows that can shatter with a blast of wind, and plant yourself in the middle of a room on the lowest floor—a basement if possible. Bathrooms are also good. Lie down and put a mattress on top of yourself and your family in case the roof comes down.

COMING HOME

Hurricane dangers don't end when the skies clear. Don't walk or drive through flooded streets, be sure to stay away from downed power lines, and don't drink tap water until authorities say it's safe. And while you will surely be eager to clean up and get back to a sense of normalcy, by all means don't try to lift that big fallen tree yourself.

CRUSHING FLORIDA
Irma caused
$67 billion in
damage in the
United States and
Caribbean.

FIERCE WINDS
After barreling through the Caribbean, Irma hit Florida on September 10, 2017, killing 134 people.

I Survived...
HURRICANE IRMA

Miami Herald reporter David Ovalle has seen a lot in his 15 years at the paper, covering everything from homicides to natural disasters. But the seasoned journalist admits that Hurricane Irma had him worried, albeit briefly.

Hurricane Irma was the 16th named storm I'd covered, so my photographer and I felt good as we drove to Key West, stocked with plenty of food, water and gas. Then my friends at the TV stations began calling to tell me their news crews were leaving. The mammoth storm, headed directly toward the tiny island, was just too dangerous. My stomach tightened. My editors wanted me to leave. So did my wife. The dread was building. That made me want to stay even more.

We, along with our Key West radio reporter, were the only journalists to remain. We hunkered down in a fortress-like former Masonic lodge, with more than a dozen Key West chefs, artists and waiters. The storm surge would blow out of the first floor, and maybe the second, we believed. The howling winds were sure to shatter the third-story windows. We ushered everyone into the stairwell—including children and dogs—to ride out this monster.

Irma was fierce, but anticlimactic in Key West fashion. After the storm knocked out my cell service and ended my live dispatches, I fell asleep on a yoga mat. I woke up to a party on the ground level. Behind glass doors, everyone drank and took photos and watched the palm trees bend under the gusts. Suddenly, a lady walked past, two dogs on a leash. Another goofball on a bicycle pedaled by, taking pics of the scenery. Within hours, as we ventured out to begin our reporting and winds still lashing Duval Street, we saw people already staggering into bars. Key West dodged the big one.

SOS 101

Since widespread power outages will hit ATMs, stash extra cash in your "go-bag" for food, gas and other supplies.

13

THE NEW NORMAL

The "Ragin' Cajun" head of the Katrina task force shares lessons learned

FAST FACT

Storms that form over water may be called hurricanes, typhoons or tropical cyclones, depending on where they are formed.

DANGEROUS TIMES High-intensity (Category 3, 4 or 5) hurricanes will become more common in coming decades.

After FEMA fumbled the response to Hurricane Katrina in New Orleans in 2005, America called in the heavy artillery. Army Lieutenant General Russel L. Honoré brought a tough, gruff, no-nonsense attitude and organizational prowess to the disaster zone. As head of Joint Task Force Katrina, the Louisiana-born commander known as the "Ragin' Cajun" turned the situation around and put the city on the road to recovery. Now retired, Honoré has lost none of his straight talk.

In the summer of 2017, Honoré got a phone call that had him steaming. It was from a friend whose daughter lived in a high-rise apartment in Houston. When the storm clouds from Hurricane Harvey deluged the city for days, the lights suddenly went out in the woman's building.

"[My friend] asked me if I could do anything," recalled Honoré, who, more than a decade after Katrina, still has many colleagues in the emergency management world. "I said: 'Let me ask you a couple of questions. Does she have a flashlight?' He said no, she had candles. I said, 'Candles! You don't want to burn the f---ing candles. They'll set the building on fire.'"

In an interview, Honoré went on like this for a while, delivering a profanity-laced diatribe about the lack of preparedness by this woman, who had a college education but no stored supplies of food, no emergency radio. She didn't even know who her neighbors were. "This is what I'm talking about," he sighed. "When you're in a disaster, you have to rely on yourself, and you and your neighbors rely on each other. Neighbors save more lives than first responders. That's a culture of preparedness."

A dozen years after he helped get New Orleans back on its feet, those were the general's marching orders for the world. Floods, hurricanes, fires, mass shootings: Get used to it. People need to prepare for disasters like they're a part of life, not something that arrives out of the blue.

"It's a glimpse into the new normal," Honoré said. "Changing weather patterns; not updating our infrastructure; not taking into account new risks; continuing to build inside flood zones; and failing to adapt building codes that make homes and buildings more resilient."

GET READY NOW "A culture of preparedness is when families and local governments make the first decisions," said Russel L. Honoré, head of Task Force Katrina.

This culture of preparedness begins at home. "You have to prepare to be your own first responder," he said. "What does that mean? You have a fire extinguisher in your kitchen. You have a first-aid kit in your house. You have three to five days' supply of water. If you can afford it, you have a backup generator."

It then expands to the neighborhood, to the workplace, to the local government, to the federal government. Take care of the small stuff and then tackle the big things: zoning changes, infrastructure investment. "If you know what your risks are and you mitigate risk by action, that is resilience," Honoré stressed. "Knowledge and preparedness overcome fear."

DESTINATION, USA
The country's unique
geography—north-south
mountains, the Gulf of
Mexico, strong jetstreams—
makes us most vulnerable
to developing the storms.

HOW TO SURVIVE A

TORNADO

IT'S NOT JUST THE WIND. IT'S ALL THAT FLYING DEBRIS

Every year tornadoes kill hundreds of people, yet many of these fatalities could be avoided. When twisters are predicted, follow reports closely on a weather radio. It'll offer more updated information than news reports. And always remember to keep low and guard against airborne debris, which causes the most deaths and injuries.

BLOWN AWAY
With winds up to
300 mph, tornado
damage can be fast
and furious.

PREVENT PROJECTILES

When a tornado hits, everything it swoops up becomes a deadly missile. To get your property twister-ready, secure anything that can become airborne, like play sets, patio furniture, barbecues, toys and other loose items. If you live in a mobile home, bolt it to a concrete foundation or chain it to beams pounded into the ground. And be sure to close all the windows in your home: Tornado winds entering an open window could lift the roof off the house.

BUILD A SHELTER

If you don't have a basement, consider digging a storm shelter. Companies manufacture steel and fiberglass underground rooms that can be installed in a day. FEMA has a helpful booklet on the subject called "Taking Shelter From the Storm: Building a Safe Room Inside Your House."

IF YOU'RE INDOORS

If you're caught inside a house that has a foundation and you don't have an underground safe place, get to the lowest floor and head into an interior room with as many walls between you and the outdoors as possible. Hallways, stairwells and walk-in closets usually provide the best protection. Mobile home residents should flee to stronger shelter; they're 15 times more likely to die in a tornado.

IF YOU'RE OUTDOORS

If you're caught outside as a tornado approaches, lie flat on the ground, preferably in a ditch, ravine or any low spot, and clasp your hands around the back of your head to protect yourself from flying debris.

IF YOU'RE IN A CAR

Drive to the nearest building that you can gain access to, like a restaurant or store. Get indoors and get low.

FAST FACT

Though Kansas may boast the most famous fictional tornado, Texas is actually America's twister capital, averaging 125 tornadoes a year.

WATER EVERYWHERE
A farm is submerged near Craig, Missouri, in March 2019, when the state was battling some of the worst flooding it had experienced in decades.

HOW TO SURVIVE A

FLOOD

WATER, WATER EVERYWHERE—AND ALL OF IT DANGEROUS. PACK UP AND FLEE TO SAFETY, BUT WATCH YOUR STEP, AND YOUR DRIVE, ALONG THE WAY

> Water: You can't live without it. Get too much, and you might not live at all. The worst natural disaster ever recorded was a flood; in 1931, a two-year drought in China ended with heavy winter snow and relentless rain, triggering a series of floods that killed 4 million people. As the residents of Houston discovered after Harvey pummeled their city in 2017, danger lurks even as the floodwaters recede, from downed power lines (especially if the flood was brought on by a storm with high winds) to disease from overflowing sewage lines and septic tanks.

COSTLY EVENTS
Floods create more
than $40 billion in
damage worldwide
each year.

TRY TO ESCAPE

Once you learn the waters are rising and you're in harm's way, get out quickly. That trickle down the gutter can become rapids within minutes that will swallow up the house and everything—and everybody—in it. Head to a shelter or a predetermined meeting place with your family.

BEWARE OF ELECTRIFIED WATER

Downed power lines can send electricity through water, and the jolt can be fatal. Stay far away from potentially electrified water, and if somebody else stumbles in, don't go in after them; you'll get shocked, too. Extend a branch or wooden stick to help them get out.

Driving through electrified water can also be deadly, so don't do it.

AIM HIGH

If debris and water thwart your evacuation plans, seek higher ground—even your house's roof. Avoid locations near streams or storm drains, if possible.

SWIM BACKWARD

If you fall into moving water, don't try to paddle away. Grab onto a branch or road sign, flop on your back and put your feet upstream to knock away debris coming toward you while shouting for help.

HEED ALARMS
Water levels can rise rapidly so get out before trouble strikes.

FAST FACT

Two-thirds of fatalities in floods are vehicle-related, when people try to drive through floodwaters and get trapped.

Get Out Of a Trapped Car

You're in your car, the floodwaters are rising and soon you'll be submerged. What should do you do? Journalist Jeff Rossen offered these tips on his Rossen to the Rescue podcast.

1 DON'T PANIC That will only waste valuable seconds you should be spending on saving your life. Collect your thoughts for a moment, and then spring into action. You can survive this.

2 ROLL DOWN THE WINDOW "It seems counterintuitive," Rossen acknowledged, but the window is your only means of escape. "Hercules could not open a car door when the water is rising against it," he said. "The pressure is too much." Move quickly before the water rises too high. This is especially true for power windows because the water may short-circuit the car's electrical system.

3 GET OUT As the water pours into the car, climb out of the window onto the roof. Look for a floating log or anything to grab onto. Rossen did a demonstration on NBC's *Today* show to prove this works. It's scary, but the alternative is worse: "Your car will become a coffin."

FIGHT FIRE ANTS

They look like rafts—but *they're alive!* After torrential rains, giant colonies of ferocious fire ants can be seen floating by in floodwaters. Fire ants have their own survival response to floods, and it's impressive. Using their special sticky feet as adhesive, they can assemble in different forms. In 25 minutes, they can pile upon themselves at water's edge to construct a structure resembling France's Eiffel Tower and stand just as strong. Most remarkably, they can hit the water in a "process analogous to the weaving of a waterproof fabric," according to a study in the science journal *PNAS*. These floating ant colonies "can look like ribbons, streamers, mats, rafts or an actual 'ball' of ants," says a Texas A&M pamphlet called "Flooding and Fire Ants: Protecting Yourself and Your Family." And they are nasty: If you disturb them, their sting can be fatal. So don't try to hose them off; they'll just cling more tightly. Instead, brush them away.

ON THE MOVE
In 2017, Houston residents took to boats to escape floodwaters.

I Survived...
HARVEY FLOODS

Brent Vasut of Houston thought the rains from Hurricane Harvey would hit Corpus Christi, which is located about three hours away. Instead, the clouds "meandered in our direction and camped out." The rain finally stopped, but the waters around his neighborhood kept rising.

We were panicking, and I felt an enormous responsibility to keep my family safe. We took 30 minutes to pack a few backpacks with valuables, passports, phones and clothing. I inflated a toy raft and threw everything on it. The kids put on rain gear, and we carried our two dogs in 3 feet of water to our car, parked at the elementary school on higher ground, about half a mile away.

After we got out, my wife said, "We need a boat. If we buy a boat with a motor, we can go to our house and get our stuff." There was an urgency to get back because there were rumors that the reservoir release would continue for weeks and authorities would limit access to the area.

So we found a sporting goods store and got a little metal fishing boat, waders and paddles.

When we went back to the house a few days later, we immediately opened the windows so air could circulate and take out the humidity.

We had 14 inches of water in our house. What was pretty gross is that it wasn't just rainwater—it was water out of the ditch, the bayou and the reservoir, and mud and sewage.

Recovery isn't as quick as everybody thinks. Flood insurance doesn't cover living expenses. All the contractors are busy. And we're supposed to continue baseball and soccer and school, and mom being mom and dad being dad, and it's tough.

MASKS MATTER
Ash and smoke can cause problems with breathing as well as visibility. Be prepared for both with protective equipment.

HOW TO SURVIVE A

VOLCANO

WHAT IF THE WORLD EXPLODES?

> On May 18, 1980, all hell broke loose in the state of Washington. There had been rumblings in the ground in Skamania County for a couple of months. Then, at 8:32 a.m. on that fateful Sunday, Mount St. Helens blew. An eruption of ash and gas rose 15 miles into the air and debris rained down for hundreds of square miles. The eruption ejected approximately 1 cubic mile of material into the sky and killed almost 60 people and thousands of animals, including deer, elk and salmon. Approximately 185 miles of highway and dozens of bridges were destroyed. The ashfall greatly affected transportation in the area. Visibility was reduced and the ash needed to be removed from the roads.

DEADLY EXPLOSION
New Zealand's most active volcano erupted in December 2019, killing more than a dozen tourists.

Removing and disposing of more than 2.4 million cubic yards of ash took over two months in some areas. When all was said and done, the eruption resulted in costs exceeding $1 billion. It was the most catastrophic volcanic eruption in the contiguous United States.

Now, imagine an eruption that makes Mount St. Helens look like a Fourth of July firecracker.

YELLOWSTONE SUPERVOLCANO

In the northwest corner of Wyoming lies a volcano roughly 1,500 square miles in size. It is referred to as a supervolcano, not because of the size but because of the explosive force it has exhibited in the past. According to the United States Geological Survey, a supervolcano is one that had an eruption that hits the magnitude of 8 on the Volcano Explosivity Index. This means it has erupted more than 240 cubic miles of material.

Experts estimate that about 2.1 million years ago, Yellowstone erupted over 1,500 cubic miles of material. The last major eruption in Yellowstone was about 640,000 years ago. While there are some who feel Yellowstone is somehow overdue for an eruption, scientists and other experts in the field say that there is no regular pattern to these events and thus they are not predictable at all. The Yellowstone Volcano Observatory has said that there are no indications that any sort of "supereruption" is imminent.

ERUPTION EFFECTS

Volcanic eruptions can send rock, ash and gases into the atmosphere. Put enough of that stuff into the sky, and not only will the air quality decline but it could affect the amount of sunlight that reaches the ground. Take Mount Tambora in Indonesia, for example. When it erupted in 1815, it sent so much material into the sky that it affected the climate for a relatively brief period.

Global temperatures were lowered. Crops failed due to the cold weather. In New Jersey, frost in June killed many plants. In parts of New York, freezing temperatures were reported throughout May and into June. This period is sometimes referred to as the Year Without a Summer.

Rarely is there just a single eruption. There is usually a series of them, of varying intensities. They are often accompanied by earthquakes, floods and mudslides in the area of the volcano. All of this adds up to potential major damage to roads and structures.

of an impending explosion, as was the case before New Zealand's White Island volcano erupted on Dec. 9, 2019, killing over a dozen people. Those who live in volcanic regions should pay attention to warnings issued by emergency management organizations. Listen for evacuation advisories and follow them as early as possible to try and get out ahead of the crowd. Driving during a heavy ashfall is not recommended. Not only is the ash slippery; it can cause serious engine damage. If you have no choice but to drive, go slow: Keep it under 35 mph.

Emergency kits should include a supply of face masks to protect the lungs from ash and other nastiness that may be floating in the air. Eye protection would also be advisable; simple swim goggles should suffice.

In the event of a large-scale eruption, such as Yellowstone, the impact could be worldwide. Food production would suffer, with potential shortages happening near and far. Areas seeing heavy ashfall would find crops buried. If a supervolcano is on your personal disaster radar, stock up on enough food and water to last several weeks.

Ash is heavy and it might build up on rooftops and need to be removed, not unlike snow accumulation that occurs in northern climates. This can be a dangerous proposition, though, so tread carefully. Whenever possible, work in teams with one person holding the ladder and keeping an eye out for hazards while the other person sweeps ash off the roof. Be sure to wear eye protection and face masks.

Massive supervolcano eruptions are extremely rare—but it only takes one to have catastrophic consequences. The good news is that preparing for such an event involves the same basic steps as preparing for most other scenarios.

supplies, such as ponds and lakes. Until it is washed away from rooftops, it will affect rainwater catchment systems. The ash can also damage engines and other machinery.

As the Mount Tambora eruption showed, if enough ash is sent into the atmosphere, it will cause major issues with farming and could bring about food shortages.

VOLCANO PREPAREDNESS

Volcanoes don't erupt without warning. History has shown there is a lead-up involving tremors, venting and other signs

HOW TO SURVIVE A
WILDFIRE

WHEN THE HEAT IS ON, PREPARE FOR THE WORST AND EVACUATE TO SAFETY. IF ALL ELSE FAILS, JUMP IN THE POOL

GET OUT
Know what evacuation route you will take in advance and have at least one backup route in mind.

> It only takes a spark. In late 2019, California's Getty, Kincade and Saddle Ridge wildfires caused billions of dollars in property damage and scorched hundreds of thousands of acres of land. Thousands of residents were displaced from their homes, and there was one civilian fatality while countless firefighters put their lives at risk. Brush fires can start any number of ways, from a careless smoker or a lightning strike to wind-whipped power lines flapping against trees. Weather conditions like low humidity, high temperatures and stubborn winds can make a small fire explode into a catastrophe. Often warnings come, but sometimes not soon enough.

ASK TOUGH QUESTIONS

When faced with a fast-moving brush fire encroaching on your location, there are two critical questions that might come up: How do I survive? And how can I keep my house safe? But to answer these questions, you might have to ask yourself two others: When should I leave? and What have I done to prepare? Authorities agree that the earlier you get out, the better. But it's also better to stay than flee at the last minute. How can you tell when it's too late to leave?

WHAT TO DO BEFORE YOU ESCAPE

The California Department of Forestry and Fire Protection (Cal Fire) recommends that you take these steps to help firefighters do their work:

On an ongoing basis, keep any wood piles and propane tanks away from your house; clear a wide zone of dry brush and dead leaves; cover attic vents with ⅛-inch mesh screens to keep embers out, and if you can, avoid having wooden decks or roofs.

When a fire does approach, shut all the windows, remove flammable curtains, shut off the gas and air conditioner and leave your lights on. And outside, move anything flammable or with propane, like grill tanks, inside. Connect your garden hoses, put a ladder at the corner of the house and turn off automated sprinklers.

Then start packing. When David Washburn evacuated Southern California's Thomas Fire in 2017, he asked himself: "What are the things that would really hurt if I lost them? And it's photos and things like that." Load your car with the trunk facing the house, and carry your keys.

WHEN TO EVACUATE

If you're advised to get out of an endangered area, do it immediately. As much as you cherish your stuff, your life (and the lives of those you love) is much more precious. The closer a fire gets, the harder it becomes to get out. Roads can get clogged with evacuees and first responders, and danger can lurk everywhere. Power lines and trees are down; people are driving like maniacs. (In late 2018, seven residents died in their vehicles trying to flee the devastating wildfires around Paradise, California, which only had one way to get out of town.) Beyond that, cajoling late evacuees or rescuing people who tried to save their homes wastes valuable resources that should be spent putting the blaze out. As you evacuate, wear long pants, a long-sleeve shirt, boots, a cap and a scarf to cover your face and eyes.

WHAT TO DO IF YOU HAVE TO STAY

On some occasions, fires move so fast it's virtually impossible to get out. Experts advise that unless you have specialized equipment and training, don't try to fight the fire. Instead, stay where you are and wait for help. Firefighters put top priority on protecting homes and may be closer than you think. It may be terrifying, but it's better than trying to outrun the flames.

DESPERATE STEPS IF THE FIRE IS ON TOP OF YOU

Dig a hole, lie in it with your feet facing the approaching flames, and cover yourself with about a foot of dirt. If possible, submerge yourself in a pool or pond.

I Survived...
THE TUBBS FIRE

As flames engulfed everything around their Santa Rosa, California, home, John and Jan Pascoe made a desperate escape into a neighbor's pool, where they stayed for six hours during the October 2017 Tubbs wildfires.

"All I saw was a red glow," Jan told the Los Angeles Times. "I said, 'John, we've got to get out of here.'" They scooped up their 17-year-old cat and a few belongings and got into their truck, but the fire was too intense to get away. Panicked, they called a dispatcher, who told them to get somewhere safe. That's when they remembered their neighbor's swimming pool. While flames engulfed the structure, the Pascoes got into the water. "I just kept going under," Jan said. "And I kept saying, 'How long does it take for a house to burn down?' We were freezing." As night fell, the temperature dropped to 40 degrees, and Jan and John were shivering. By morning, six hours later, they felt safe enough to leave the pool. Their house, and their neighbor's house, was gone, but they were luckier than another couple. During that same destructive fire, Armando and Carmen Berriz, a married couple of 55 years, got in a swimming pool, also in Santa Rosa, to escape the flames. "They went hand-in-hand, together, and jumped into the pool," daughter Monica Ocon told CNN. Armando, survived, but his wife died in her husband's arms.

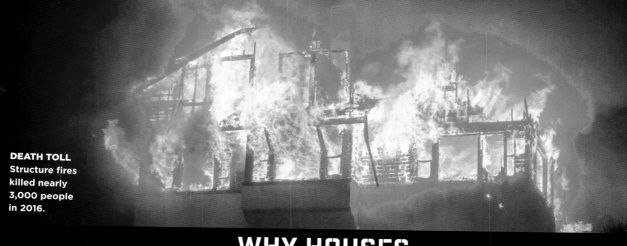

DEATH TOLL
Structure fires killed nearly 3,000 people in 2016.

WHY HOUSES EASILY CATCH FIRE

It often happens at night. A faulty portable heater sets off a fire that spreads quickly. How much time do you have to get out of the house? According to a Red Cross survey, most people think they have five to 10 minutes. In reality, it's only two minutes. House fires kill nearly seven people a day. The most common hazards are malfunctioning cooking equipment, unattended candles, electrical connections and smoldering cigarettes or cigars. And yet many homeowners have not drafted escape plans, installed smoke detectors or purchased fire extinguishers. Know what to do, before it's too late.

INSTALL SMOKE ALARMS
You can increase your odds of surviving a house fire by 50 percent just by installing smoke alarms. Put them on every floor, inside each bedroom, and be sure to check them monthly by pushing the battery test button.

PRACTICE EVACUATING
Gather up the family and form a plan for getting out of the house and then reconnecting after a fire. The plan should cover at least two ways of exiting the house. Then practice with regular fire drills.

FIRES BURN QUICKLY
If the fire is larger than a small kitchen blaze that you can extinguish yourself, evacuate immediately, following your plan.

GET LOW
Smoke kills more people than fire, and smoke inhalation causes disorientation and unconsciousness. As smoke rises, crawl out of the house and cover your mouth and nose with a towel or shirt. Before opening a door, check for smoke underneath coming from another room. Close all doors behind you as you leave to slow the spread.

IF YOU'RE TRAPPED
Call 911 if you can get to your phone. Close doors and windows. Shove towels or clothing—wet, if possible—under doors to block smoke from entering. If you're on a higher story, hang a sheet out of the window to let firefighters know where you are, then close the window to keep out air that fans the flames.

IF YOU'RE ON FIRE
The experts advise: "Stop, drop and roll." Get to the ground, cover your face with your hands, and roll around to snuff out flames on your clothes.

MAKING WAVES
A 9.0 earthquake off the coast of Japan in 2011 sent water crashing over seawalls in Miyako. The quake and tsunami killed 16,000 people.

Nature Strikes Back

HOW TO SURVIVE A

TSUNAMI

HEAD FOR HIGHER GROUND OR HOLD ON FOR DEAR LIFE

> Japanese for "harbor wave," a tsunami brings monster waves from underwater earthquakes, landslides and volcanic eruptions and can inflict devastation of biblical proportions. One of the worst natural disasters ever was the fourth century eastern Mediterranean tsunami that killed a half-million people. If one is headed your way, be ready to move—now.

KNOW WHEN IT'S COMING

If you live in a tsunami zone, make a habit of following the news so you don't miss bulletins about an earthquake or other tsunami-triggering event. Have a plan in place with your family that includes departure routes and a meet-up site.

WHEN TO GET OUT

If you feel the earthquake, don't wait for an official evacuation order. Tsunami waves travel at jetliner speed. You may have only minutes before a 10-foot wall of water crashes over you. Don't be lulled into a false sense of security if the beach has a calm low tide. An arriving tsunami can often suck water away from shorelines and expose reefs. This is a warning sign that disaster is close.

FIND HIGHER GROUND

If the quake happened far out to sea and you have extra time to evacuate, gather up your pets, pack some belongings and move to a spot at least 100 feet above sea level or 2 miles inland. Avoid rivers and streams that could turn into raging torrents. You may be better off evacuating on foot so you don't get caught in a traffic jam.

HANG TIGHT

Climb onto a roof or up a tree and stay there for several hours. Even if the waters recede, another tsunami may hit. Otherwise, grab onto anything strong you can find, from a tree to a street lamp, and hold on as tightly as you can. In a worst-case scenario, latch on to a floating log or other debris to use as a life preserver.

POWERFUL & DESTRUCTIVE For many tsunamis, the only warning is a report of an earthquake, meaning there may be just minutes to escape.

พื้นที่เสี่ยงภัยคลื่นยักษ์

TSUNAMI HAZARD ZONE

**IN CASE OF EARTHQUAKE, GO
TO HIGH GROUND OR INLAND**

เมื่อเกิดแผ่นดินไหว ให้หนีห่าง
จากชายหาดและขึ้นที่สูงโดยเร็ว

เทศบาลตำบลเกาะลันตาใหญ่

MUNITY OFFICE

ยา →

ILLAGE

I Survived...
THE INDIAN OCEAN TSUNAMI

Petra Nemcova heard the screams and saw the bodies and debris float by after a tsunami walloped Thailand on December 26, 2004. The Czech supermodel suffered a broken pelvis but survived by clinging to a tree for eight painful hours.

"I thought, well, if I'm meant to go, so be it and I made my peace with what was happening," she told the *Telegraph*. "And then, as soon as I let go and accepted my fate, I was back above the water and could breathe again. I will never know how that happened."

Among the 230,000 people who perished in a series of tsunamis in Southeast Asia triggered by the third-largest earthquake ever recorded was her photographer boyfriend, Simon Atlee. Sadly, he was swept away as the couple was walking on the beach. More than 13 years later, Nemcova still hears the cries. She founded the Happy Hearts Charity, which builds disaster-resilient schools in nine countries. "I was blessed to survive a near-death experience," she said when she received an award in 2017 from the Japan Society in New York. "We cannot control nature, but we can control the actions we take."

FEELS LIKE AN ETERNITY
The 2017 temblor lasted 20 terrifying seconds for people in Mexico City and surrounding areas.

SOS 101

Because earthquakes kick up so much dust, experts advise that you stock your emergency kit with goggles and particle masks, along with the usual supplies of water, canned food, first-aid materials, a battery-operated radio and vital documents.

HOW TO SURVIVE AN

EARTHQUAKE

WHEN THE BIG ONE STRIKES, YOU NEED TO BE READY TO SHAKE, RATTLE AND ROLL WITH IT

> The floodwaters from Hurricane Irma (which hit the Caribbean and Florida) were still receding when Mother Nature reminded the world she wasn't finished. On September 19, 2017, a 7.1-magnitude earthquake struck central Mexico, killing 370 people and injuring thousands more while leaving entire blocks in rubble. It was a stark reminder that earthquakes—unlike hurricanes, which are tracked by weather radar—strike out of nowhere. Survival relies on readiness and knowledge. As the Centers for Disease Control says, "Surviving an earthquake and reducing its health impact requires preparation, planning and practice." That means stocking up on supplies, earthquake-proofing the house, and drafting a family emergency plan so you'll know what to do when the ground starts moving.

IF YOU'RE INSIDE

The best advice: "Drop, cover and hold." That means getting under a strong table or desk, or against a wall if you can't get to that furniture; protecting your head and neck against falling objects and tumbling debris; and making yourself as small as possible. Get away from fireplaces that can collapse into a pile of bricks, and windows that can shatter. If you're in a high-rise, don't get on an elevator.

IF YOU'RE OUTSIDE

Try to get away from power lines or bridges and into a wide open space, which is the safest place you can be in a quake. Don't go into a building. If you're in an arena or sports stadium, stay in your seat and cover your head and neck with your hands until the shaking stops. Then evacuate slowly and carefully, following all official instructions.

IF YOU'RE IN A CAR

Pull over, making sure you're away from overpasses or power lines, then stay there.

Your car serves as your best protection against falling objects. The exception is if you're in a multilevel parking garage, where metal and steel are no match against falling concrete. Get out of the car and crouch next to it.

TRAPPED UNDER RUBBLE

Pause and collect yourself. Panic will only make the situation worse. Resist the urge to thrash around; that will kick up dust. And try not to yell, which can only cause you to choke on that dust. If you have your phone, dial 911. Tap on a pipe or wall to signal your location to rescuers. Don't light a match.

AFTER A QUAKE

Wait until the shaking completely stops. If you are home, and it is safe to get around, unplug major appliances, and shut off gas and electricity. Look for a clear escape route and leave the building. Make sure you and those around you have no injuries. Help rescuers if it is safe to do so. Stay clear of downed power lines and debris. And be on the alert for aftershocks, staying far away from exterior walls and windows.

PROTECT BREAKABLES

It doesn't take a lot of shaking to cause a lot of injuries or damage. Vases, figurines and furniture—they all can go flying in an earthquake. To save these valuables, and prevent them from hitting you or others, affix shelf units to walls with screws into the studs or with L-brackets or special earthquake "straps." This will keep these top-heavy pieces from collapsing onto the floor—or on you. Then take a couple of small steps to save a lot of grief later on.

1 ANCHOR OBJECTS A putty-like product known as museum wax can be placed on the bottoms of smaller objects to keep them in place.

2 USE NONSLIP MATS Heavy objects with a low center of gravity can be placed on mats that keep them from sliding around.

3 KEEP LARGE ITEMS LOW Put heavier, larger pieces on low shelves. They'll tumble a shorter distance.

ON SHAKY GROUND
The 2016 quake caused lots of damage, but no lives were lost.

I Survived...
THE CHRISTCHURCH EARTHQUAKE

Web designer Sarah Areina grew up in New Zealand and thought she was ready for an earthquake, having done duck-and-cover drills as a kid in school. But when Areina and her partner visited Christchurch, on the island's east coast, on Valentine's Day, 2016, she got a real wake-up call. A 5.7-magnitude quake collapsed seaside cliffs, sent shipping containers tumbling and knocked rocks down to within feet of surfers, but amazingly caused no fatalities.

We do earthquake drills from the age of about 4 here. We get around 14,000 earthquakes a year, with about 20 over 5.0 on the Richter scale. That's what you get for colonizing a set of islands in the Pacific that sits right on a fault line.

I went out by myself to have a coffee at the mall. As I finished, things started shaking. But I'd been in small earthquakes before so I felt I was OK.

The ground was moving up and down. I first thought: How bad is this, a 2 or a 7? I saw people

getting under tables. That's when I went 'Oh sh--' and jumped under a table. I've never been so terrified in my life. I held onto the table leg while I jolted up and down. I didn't even have time to wonder if I would die because the fear was stopping thoughts. I just had feelings.

When the shaking stopped, everyone had all gone. I was left crying under a table. I found the only other crying person and we stuck together. For me, it's a reminder of how fragile life can be.

SIGNAL FOR HELP
Wearing an
avalanche beacon
can help rescuers
find you before
it's too late.

HOW TO SURVIVE AN

AVALANCHE

THE SNOW CAN SWEEP YOU AWAY
LIKE A RAGING RIVER

> You're taking a long hike through a snowy wonderland, and suddenly you hear it. A crack, a rumble, then a roar. The ground begins to shudder. In seconds, the whole mountain gives way, taking you with it. Surviving an avalanche requires quick thinking and a calm demeanor.

FALLEN HEROES
At least 23 rescue workers died after being buried under an avalanche in eastern Turkey in February 2020.

BE PREPARED

Backcountry snow hikers should always bring an avalanche beacon, a small radio that'll signal your location to rescuers. It's also wise to take an emergency shovel and a helmet that could protect you from a blow to the head. Some hikers and skiers now carry air bags; with a pull of a string, one or two big balloons inflate that can help keep you atop an avalanche. And be sure to take an avalanche training course, because you'll need to be able to think and act fast.

JUMP AWAY

Since your weighted footsteps probably triggered the avalanche in the first place—90 percent of avalanche accidents are caused by the victim or somebody in their party—look for the fissure, then leap upslope and keep going. If that doesn't work, try running to the side away from the avalanche, as if you were in a riptide.

GRAB OR "SWIM"

If you start to get swept downhill, think of the avalanche as like being caught in rapids. Grab

FAST
FACT

Avalanches
can hit 35 mph
within five
seconds and
top out at
250 mph.

onto something big, like a tree, or crouch behind a rock. If that fails, try to "swim" your way to the top by thrusting and kicking as if caught in the surf. As awkward as it sounds, try to keep one arm skyward at all times. This will help you keep track of which way is up. It may also end up poking out of the snow, giving rescuers a lock on your location.

OPEN AN AIR HOLE

If you end up buried under the snow, you need two things. The first is air. Start spitting,

as this will begin to melt snow, opening a pocket so you can breathe. You'll also need to know which way is up. Pay attention to which way your spit drips—that's down. Start trying to climb in the opposite direction.

CALMLY WAIT

You'll have about 30 minutes of air from that little pocket. It may not sound like much, but that could be enough. Rescuers may be close by. Don't waste breath on screaming until you hear them above.

FROZEN IN PLACE
The 2011 Groundhog Day blizzard buried Chicago in up to 2 feet of snow and brought 60 mph winds.

HOW TO SURVIVE A
BLIZZARD

WHEN THE TEMPERATURES PLUNGE, THE MOST IMPORTANT THING TO DO IS LEARN HOW TO KEEP YOUR COOL

It seems counterintuitive: Global warming could be making winters colder. Rising temperatures and melting ice in the Arctic appear to be wreaking havoc on weather patterns in much of the Northern Hemisphere. This may account for the freezing of the Hudson River in New York in the winter of 2015—the first time that has happened since the Little Ice Age of the 1700s and early 1800s. The winter of 2013 to 2014 set cold records in the Midwest. So look for more—and more brutal—blizzards and ice storms like those that haven't been seen since the Great Blizzard of 1888, which forced nearly half the United States indoors under 5 feet of snow. For those trapped in sub-freezing conditions, paralyzing wind and blinding snow, the key to surviving the cold relies on preparation—and not getting too hot under the collar when the snow starts piling up.

BLOWN AWAY
It's dangerous to be
outdoors in a blizzard—
hypothermia can come
on very quickly.

**FAST
FACT**

What makes a
blizzard? Temps
below 20 degrees;
visibility of less than
a quarter-mile; winds
of at least 35 mph.
And snow, lots
of snow.

BE PATIENT

When the weather outside is frightful, there's no better place than the warm indoors. But if you do find yourself trapped in a blizzard, either on foot or in a car, patience isn't just a virtue; it may be a lifesaver. Do what you can to draw the rescuers to you, while staying hydrated to fend off hypothermia and frostbite. And, of course, keep as warm as possible.

TRAPPED OUTSIDE

There's a good chance somebody has reported you missing and they'll be looking for you. Stay put in the snow unless you see a building nearby, and if you do, carefully walk toward it, tossing a rock or stick ahead to check the snowy terrain. Stomp out the words "Help" or "SOS" in the snow, then fill it in with rocks or twigs so rescuers can see it. Hopefully, you've brought some water; you'll need five ounces every hour to stay hydrated. Don't eat snow, though; it'll lower your body temperature.

STUCK IN A CAR

You're probably in the best shelter you can find for the time being, so don't leave. Drink plenty of water if you have it, but don't go outside to urinate—use a bottle or plastic bag. Exposing that much of yourself to the cold could bring on hypothermia. Turn off the engine; a snow-clogged tailpipe can fill the car with deadly carbon monoxide from the exhaust. Only go outside to put a plastic bag or colorful cloth on the antenna to let rescuers know the car is occupied, and turn on the inside light. Keep warm by covering up with anything you can find in the car, from newspapers to road maps.

Build An Igloo

So simple looking yet so perfectly engineered, the igloo stands as one of the best shelters for punishing Arctic environments. Over generations, indigenous people mastered the art of igloo building, along with some tricks, like an underground entrance.

1 SIZE Tie a cord to a stick and use it to etch a circle no more than 10 feet in diameter in flat, hard-packed snow. (Any bigger requires a perfect dome and special tools.)

2 WALLS Cut snow blocks, each 3 feet long by 15 inches high, from inside the circle. Don't use the powdery top layers of snow, but the lower, harder stuff. Start building the blocks in a spiral formation, like a ramp, with each new layer tipping slightly inward. Get additional blocks from outside the igloo. Water down the outside and let it freeze, since ice is stronger than snow.

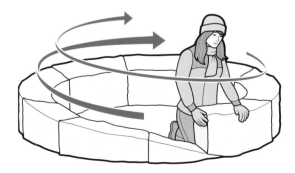

3 ENTRANCE Dig a hole outside the igloo, then tunnel in to maintain maximum heat.

Keep the hole open to allow ventilation, and cut another vent hole in the wall for circulation.

SHIFTING SKIES
The weather can change quickly, so get to shelter ASAP if you hear thunder or see a lightning flash.

HOW TO SURVIVE A

LIGHTNING STRIKE

COMPLACENCY KILLS. MANY DIE FROM LIGHTNING, THINKING IT WILL NEVER HIT THEM. HEED THE WARNING: "WHEN THUNDER ROARS, GO INDOORS"

> It's true what they say. The chances of getting struck by lightning are extremely slim: one in 600,000. But don't be reckless. Lightning is one of the leading weather-related causes of death, killing 24,000 people a year worldwide, often because they fail to take these simple precautions.

ALL LIT UP
Lightning strikes often
cause wildfires and
can lead to significant
property damage.

FOLLOW THE 30/30 RULE

When thunderstorms are in the forecast, stay in your home or office. "There is no safe place outside when thunderstorms are in the area," says the National Weather Service. "If you hear thunder, you are likely within striking distance of the storm." To gauge how close you are to danger, start counting after you see a lightning flash. If thunder roars before you reach 30, you need to stay protected until 30 minutes after the last blast of thunder.

STAY INDOORS

The safest place to be is in a substantial building with wiring and plumbing that will carry lightning's electrical charge away from you. Stay away from pipes, faucets, computers, landline phones, windows and doors. Don't lean against concrete walls or lie on concrete floors; they may contain wire mesh or hide pipes within.

BE CAREFUL OUTDOORS

If you get caught outside, stay away from open fields or the tops of hills and ridges. Seek protection under a stand of trees, staying closest to the shortest ones, and avoid isolated trees, telephone poles, barbed-wire fences and windmills. Small shelters like huts and picnic covers may be lightning targets because they tend to be isolated. If you feel your hairs stand on end, that could mean a lightning strike is imminent. Don't lie flat on the ground; instead, crouch on the balls of your feet and cover your ears to protect your hearing from the thunder.

A CAR CAN PROTECT YOU

If you're in a hardtop vehicle, stay put (a convertible is not safe), but don't touch any metal. It's a myth that the rubber from the tires will protect you—just ask any farmer struck by lightning while driving a tractor with big tires.

GET OUT OF THE WATER

If you're out for a swim, be it in a lake, stream, river or ocean, immediately get out, because the water will conduct electricity. If you're in a small boat with no cabin, head for shore. Large boats with cabins (particularly those outfitted with lightning protection systems) offer protection. But don't touch metal or plumbing fixtures. If you're scuba diving and your boat has no cabin, dive deeply for as long as is safe.

DON'T ASSEMBLE IN A GROUP

Spread out and don't hold hands—the electricity can carry through your bodies.

LUCKY TO BE ALIVE
Jason Bunch, 17, of Castle Rock, Colorado, was struck by lightning while mowing the lawn in July 2017. His iPod acted as a conductor as the electricity followed the cord from his ear to his right knee, where the unit was stashed in his shorts pocket. Bunch suffered burns to his face, hands and feet and lost hearing in his right ear.

CHAPTER 02

TERRORISM AND CRIME

> A lone gunman perched in a window high above the Las Vegas Strip uses high-powered rifles to mow down concertgoers. When man's inhumanity seems boundless, arm yourself with the right knowledge to react quickly should you find yourself in a mass shooting, vehicle-ramming attack, terrorist bombing or home invasion.

You may not think of yourself as a hero, but if all else fails, fighting back against a shooter offers the best chances for survival. Think as a group. Experts say two to four people can subdue even a heavily armed attacker.

MODERN TRAGEDY Six of the deadliest mass shootings in U.S. history have happened in the past 10 years, according to Giffords Law Center.

HOW TO SURVIVE A

MASS
SHOOTING

WHEN THE BULLETS FLY, FAST THINKING AND SWIFT ACTION CAN SAVE YOUR LIFE

A Walmart in El Paso, Texas. A high school in Parkland, Florida. A concert in Las Vegas. Another new mass shooting seems to happens every few days. Survival comes down to preparation and reaction. Dr. Pete Blair, a professor of criminal justice and director of the Advanced Law Enforcement Rapid Response Training Center at Texas State University, stresses these three words: "Avoid. Deny. Defend."

RIGHT LANE
MUST
TURN RIGHT

NO PARKING ANY TIME

FBI

131

AVOID AT ALL COSTS

"The best thing you can do is get away from the attacker as fast as you can," says Blair, encouraging people to think creatively to do so—for instance, breaking a window to escape outside. That means responding quickly to danger signs. If you hear something that may be gunfire, don't dismiss it as firecrackers. Start moving now because every second matters.

Identifying secondary exits beforehand, at any location where you commonly spend time—whether it's the grocery store, theater or workplace—will help you take better action in the moment. "If you've thought about it a little bit, then you can get past the

denial phase more quickly, and you'll have a script to follow," Blair says.

"I've gotten in the habit of walking into a store and identifying the exits. It's an easy habit to get into, and it might save your life, whether there's a shooting or a fire or other emergency."

CREATE A BARRIER

If there's no way to avoid the attacker, try to keep them away from you. Seek shelter behind a locked or barricaded door, or otherwise create a barrier between you and the attacker—it could save your life, since most gunmen will move on to more accessible targets.

HIGH SCHOOL HORROR
Two students armed with assault rifles and bombs killed 12 students and a teacher before taking their own lives in Columbine, Colorado, in 1999.

RIGHT LANE
MUST
TURN RIGHT

FINAL MOMENTS
Columbine shooters Eric Harris and Dylan Klebold were caught on security cameras 11 minutes before their suicides.

I. 11:57:20 03 AM   04/20/99

Still, it's not as ideal as finding a way to flee. "In general, it's a good idea not to be seen, but the drawback is that if you do it in a way that doesn't give you a way out, then you've limited how you can escape," Blair says.

He also cautioned against the immobility of playing dead, since shooters will often fire at bodies more than once. "You don't want to make yourself an easy target," he adds, noting that moving targets are obviously harder to hit than stationary targets.

FIGHT FOR YOUR LIFE

If you feel like you've got no way to escape, don't just throw in the towel—be ready to defend yourself. "Don't just let them kill you," Blair says, noting that people have successfully stopped attackers in about one out of five cases. Your best chance to take down the shooter is when they stop to reload. There is strength in numbers, so try to recruit others who will be ready to pounce with you to disarm the shooter.

If you are carrying a gun or can get to one quickly, keep in mind that it's best not to start shooting back unless it is an absolute last resort. In the chaos of a mass shooting, police may confuse you with the assailant, or you may accidentally hit innocent people.

DON'T LIVE IN FEAR

It's advantageous to consider what you would do in a life-threatening situation, in the same way it's crucial for students to practice fire drills and learn to "stop, drop and roll," Blair says. But you should not live in fear. Peace of mind will come from knowing what to do. "As attention-grabbing as the active shooter events are—keep it in perspective," he said. "These events are rare. That's not to say that you shouldn't be prepared, but people tend to have a higher level of fear about these than they should."

SUTHERLAND SPRINGS
The 26 crosses placed just outside the crime scene tape memorialize the victims of the First Baptist Church shooting on November 9, 2017, in Texas.

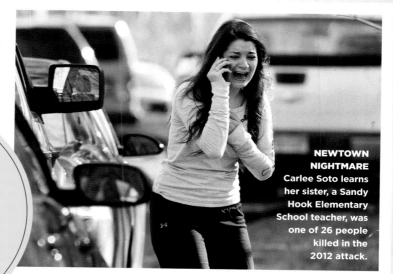
NEWTOWN NIGHTMARE Carlee Soto learns her sister, a Sandy Hook Elementary School teacher, was one of 26 people killed in the 2012 attack.

61

FESTIVAL HORROR
Las Vegas shooter Stephen Paddock fired more than 1,000 rounds of ammunition on the unsuspecting crowds.

THE LAS VEGAS SHOOTING

Sydney Cueva, 22, a California State University, Long Beach student, was snapping a selfie with her mother during Jason Aldean's performance at the Route 91 Harvest, a country music festival, when a hail of bullets started raining down from a hotel across the street. The October 1, 2017, massacre left 58 dead and 546 wounded.

At the first sound of gunfire, everyone got down and covered one another. We couldn't see where the shots were coming from. We didn't know if the gunman was inside the concert venue. We didn't know if there were multiple shooters. We didn't know which way to run, but we knew we couldn't stay where we were.

So, like everyone around us, we waited for breaks in the gunfire. Then we'd sprint in our cowgirl boots as far as we could toward the nearest exit. When the firing would start again, we'd get back on the ground and huddle up.

Everyone was kind of doing the same thing, and everyone just wanted the hell out of there. It's crazy, but everyone was diving and getting up at the same time, and people were helping each other and picking each other up.

As we made our escape, we saw people who were hurt, or worse, and we passed a security guard drenched in blood from helping victims.

We ran by a girl, and I think she was dead, but my mom wanted to go help her. I grabbed my mom and said, "We have to go." I couldn't stop thinking about my mom or her friends, who are like family.

One of my mom's friends had a forceful hold on my ponytail so that we wouldn't get separated, and it hurt, but it was good to feel she was there. When you are with someone you love in a situation like that, you care more about their life than your own. Somehow, I stayed calm and focused. I didn't shut down—I carried on, which taught me something about myself that I'm proud of.

Our group made it out safe, and it's hard to believe we were that lucky. We watched the news reports afterward in numbed silence, in shock that so many had been killed, and in pain because we couldn't understand why it happened.

We still don't have answers about why the gunman did what he did. All we can do now is cope with the memories.

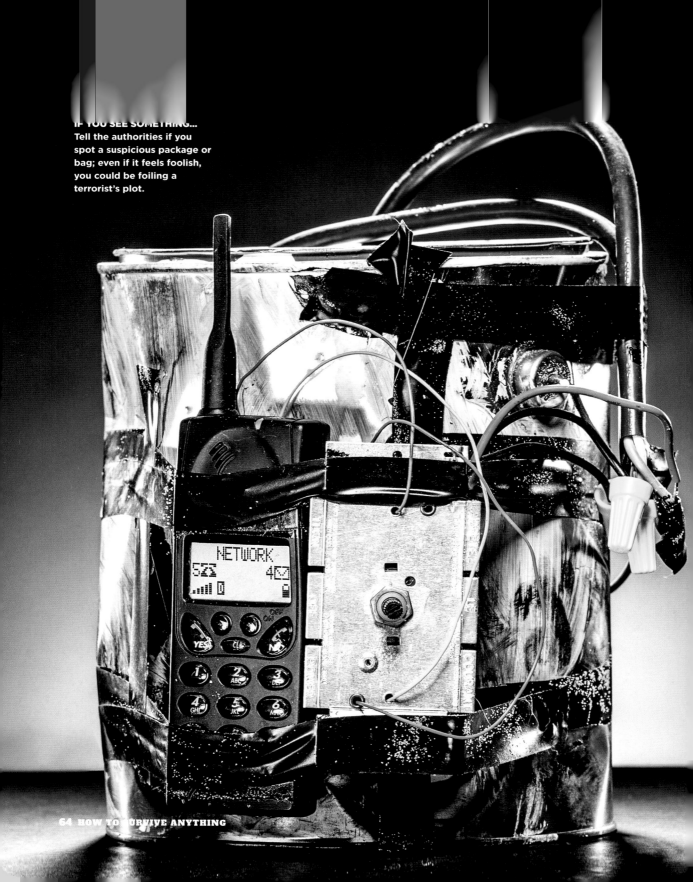

IF YOU SEE SOMETHING...
Tell the authorities if you spot a suspicious package or bag; even if it feels foolish, you could be foiling a terrorist's plot.

NETWORK

HOW TO SURVIVE A

BOMB ATTACK

SAVE YOURSELF FROM A BLAST, THEN WATCH OUT FOR THE NEXT ONE

> Red wire or blue? You've seen it in countless movies: As the clock ticks, our hero has to decide which wire to snip, with sweaty hands, to defuse a bomb. But in real life, bomb-makers aren't so courteous as to color-code the wires. Real bombs are more primitive and in some ways more unpredictable and deadly. By the time that bomb goes off, you will have to be responsible for yourself.

BE ON THE LOOKOUT

If you see an unattended bag or box, immediately alert police and move away. Report suspicious-looking people, like somebody wearing a big coat in the heat of summer. Don't open a package that arrives at your home or business if it lacks postage and a return address that you recognize. Nearly all package bombs are placed, not delivered through the regular mail, according to the U.S. Postal Service.

DUCK AND COVER

When a bomb goes off, crawl under a strong table if possible to protect against falling debris, and lie flat on the ground to avoid getting hit by shrapnel from additional blasts. Cover your mouth and nose with any sort of cloth you have to ward against harmful dust and smoke. If you get trapped, alert rescuers by tapping on a nearby object. Try not to yell, because you will inhale the toxins.

MAKE AN ESCAPE

Wait at least one minute. If you don't hear any more explosions and if the rubble stops falling, get out of the area, taking great care with each step. Don't waste time looking for your cellphone or purse. Avoid elevators and stay away from windows. Watch for fire. If there's smoke, stay low to the ground to protect against smoke inhalation. Keep away from crowds that may serve as a secondary target and avoid unattended cars and trucks that may contain more bombs. Stay at least 200 yards away from the bombing site. Follow instructions from emergency personnel and alert them to trapped or injured people. Check yourself for injuries and seek treatment if needed.

WHAT THE BOMB SQUAD REALLY DOES

Rather than defuse an explosive like they do in Hollywood movies, bomb squads will clear out the area and disarm or weaken the bomb by simply shooting it with a rifle or high-power water cannon. Often, robots are sent in to do this work. The device also may be transported to a chamber where it's destroyed. When a bomb is located in a tight space, the experts in the big blast-proof suits are called in.

FAST FACT

The worst bombing in U.S. history was the April 19, 1995 attack on the Oklahoma City federal building that killed 169, including 19 children.

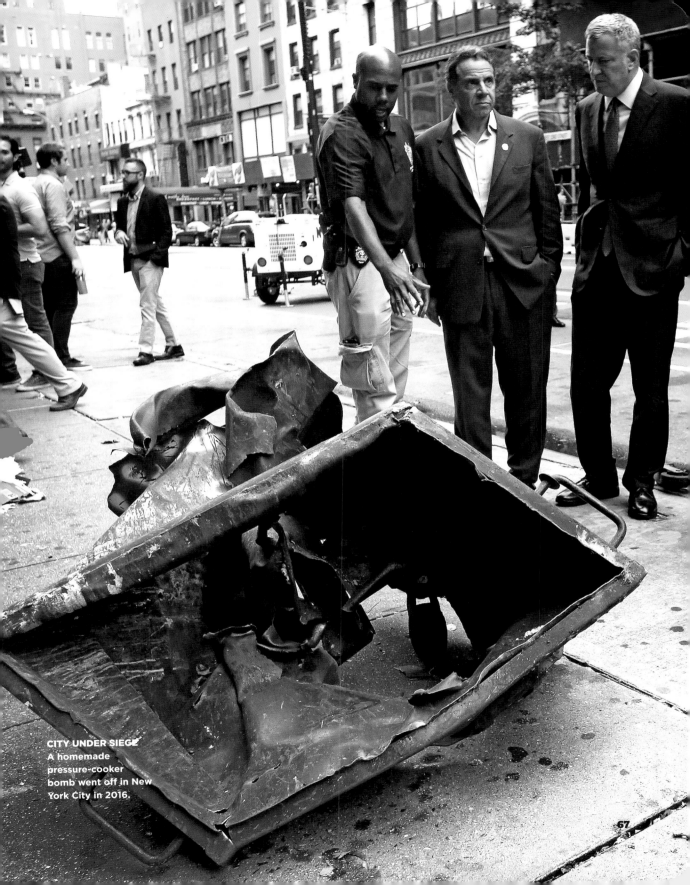

CITY UNDER SIEGE
A homemade
pressure-cooker
bomb went off in New
York City in 2016.

LOW-TECH TERROR
Cars and trucks can easily turn
into weapons by those who
wish to inflict harm, especially
when used in crowded places.

Terrorism and Crime

HOW TO SURVIVE A

VEHICLE RAMMING

WHEN TRUCKS AND VANS BECOME WEAPONS, KNOW WHAT TO DO IN A CROWD

> On the evening of July 14, 2016, a terrorist plowed a 20-ton rented cargo truck into crowds celebrating Bastille Day on a beachfront promenade in Nice, France. With 86 people dead and more than 400 injured, it was one of the worst cases of an unsettling trend—using vehicles as weapons of terror. In 2017 alone, attacks were carried out in New York City, London, Stockholm, Barcelona and Edmonton, Canada. Going after what experts call "soft" or "medium" targets—large groups of people gathered in open spaces accessible by streets—vehicle attacks are difficult to stop once set in motion. While barriers and increased security help, the key to survival in a group often rests on how an individual acts.

BE AWARE
Take the time to look and listen. Don't ignore a vehicle that seems to be moving too quickly or erratically. Listen for the sound of a revving engine. Even a couple of seconds of warning could make a major difference. Avoid the middle of a crowd; keep on the fringes. If the event you're attending has a dedicated area blocked off by barriers or police cars, stick to that location—but be sure to stay away from temporary stages or viewing platforms that can be toppled.

TRY TO ESCAPE
When a vehicle careens into the crowd, take a split second to gauge its direction of attack and then run the other way. Do not just stand there. Seek cover behind a block wall, a large tree, around the back of a building or in an alcove. If you can get inside a building, get to a place as far from the street as possible. Avoid windows. The safest place to be is inside.

BE A HERO LATER
Even when the vehicle comes to a stop, great danger still exists. This may not be the only attack. The driver may jump out shooting, or set off a bomb. There may be a second vehicle on its way. Listen for gunfire or another vehicle. When the action appears to have subsided, carefully assess the situation. See if authorities have responded. Check yourself for injuries. In all the excitement you may have gotten hurt without knowing it. Only when everything appears completely safe should you help others.

FAST FACT

In 2017, the Transportation Security Administration (TSA) warned truck-rental companies to be on the lookout for potential terrorists.

FATAL SHOOT-OUT
The suspect in the Nice attack was shot and killed by authorities.

MAXIMUM CARNAGE
Terrorists are drawn to pedestrian-only locations in order to kill the highest number of people with vehicles.

ON THE RISE
Vehicle-ramming attacks
have grown in popularity
among terrorists because
they take little skill and can
cause many casualties.

SEVEN-SECOND RULE
Self-defense experts say
it takes just seven seconds
for a criminal to pick his
or her next victim.

FAST FACT

Which U.S. city
has the highest
murder rate? It's
St. Louis, where the
188 murders in 2019
added up to a rate of
60.9 killings per
100,000 people.

HOW TO SURVIVE A

VIOLENT CRIME

EVIL LURKS AMONG US. LEARN HOW TO DEFEND YOURSELF FROM KILLERS, RAPISTS AND ROBBERS

> Violent crimes are offenses that involve force or the threat of force and include murder and non-negligent manslaughter, forcible rape, robbery and aggravated assault. There are steps you can take to prevent falling victim to an evil predator. "Before people become violent, they often provide others with signs that they are on a path—or continuum—of violence," according to the authors of *Staying Alive: How to Act Fast and Survive Deadly Encounters*. And if that fails, as a last resort, know how to fight back to thwart an attack.

BE AWARE OF YOUR SURROUNDINGS
We mean, really, really aware. "Awareness is the greatest and most important tool in your self-defense toolbox," Nathan Corliss, author of *An Idiots Guide to Self Defense*, has said. "How do you train awareness? Many will say, 'I'm always aware.' Are you? Do you notice peculiar behavior? Do you pay attention to where a person's hands are? Or what's in their hands? Do you notice that person who seems to get closer in a crowd, the person next to you? Did that person look at you when you entered the elevator?" Corliss advises to scan your environment, looking for anything or anyone that stands out. Also, take notice of all exits, and pay attention to all people—from their clothing to their mannerisms and body language.

SELF-DEFENSE TIPS

Sometimes, despite even the best efforts to avoid or evade the bad guy, you may have to put up a fight. Here's what to do:

MAKE SOME NOISE
Don't just scream; choose words that make it clear that you are in trouble—like "Rape! Attacker! 911! Help!" They make it clear to others that something is very wrong and you need help.

MESS WITH HIS VISION
Su Ericksen, author of the Self-Defense for Women websites, suggests gouging, poking or scratching the attacker's eyes with your fingers or knuckles. By temporarily interfering with his vision, you may be able to make a run for it.

GO FOR HIS WEAK SPOTS
If an attacker has a hold on you, apply force at his thumb. It's where his grip will be the weakest. If you're facing him, kick him in the groin as hard as you can, or push the heel of the palm of your hand to his nose or throat.

USE YOUR LEGS
If the bad guy has you down on your back, use your legs—they're your largest muscle group—to push him off you.

CARRY A SELF-DEFENSE KEY CHAIN
Placing keys between your fingers in order to throw a punch isn't an effective means of self-defense, says Jarrett Arthur, founder of M.A.M.A. (Mothers Against Malicious Acts). The keys will be pushed back toward your palm upon impact. She suggests something like the My Kitty Self Defense Personal Keychain: You slip your fingers through the eye holes, and the ears act as weapons. This weapon, however, will do no good buried in your bag or pocket. When walking alone, have the key chain in your hand.

ARM YOURSELF
Mace and pepper sprays are effective only if you can get to them. Try one on a key chain.

In order to be truly aware, you must avoid distractions. That means not checking your Instagram feed, chatting on your phone or listening to music. A distracted person becomes a prime target for a predator.

CREATE A DISTRACTION

If a violent criminal does come after you, your first line of defense should be distraction. While the culprit may be scary as hell, chances are he is dumb. "Men with low intelligence may be more likely to resort to evolutionarily familiar means of competition for resources (theft rather than full-time employment) and mating opportunities (rape rather than computer dating), and not to comprehend fully the consequences of criminal behavior," Satoshi Kanazawa said in *Psychology Today.* A successful distraction—like when California resident Julie Dragland faked a seizure in September 2017 on a train in California when a would-be robber demanded her wallet and phone, or her life—may either get the assailant to flee or allow you time to escape.

GET OUTTA THERE

After distracting the criminal, get away as quickly as possible. No matter how tempting, do not hide in a bathroom or other isolated location. Get near others—run into a store or a restaurant—and call 911 as soon as possible.

KNOW YOUR RISK

It can help you avoid becoming the victim of a violent crime

78%
The percentage of murder victims who are male

89%
The percentage of killers who are men

43%
The percentage of people murdered during arguments or over love triangles, nearly twice the percentage of people killed during felonies like robbery or burglary

53%
The percentage of people killed by someone they know, like a neighbor, friend or boyfriend

20-24
The overwhelming number of murder victims are between these ages

43%
The percentage of robberies that take place in the street. The majority of muggings happen between the hours of 8 p.m. and 3 a.m.

71%
The percentage of murders committed using a gun

89%
The percentage of robberies committed using a gun

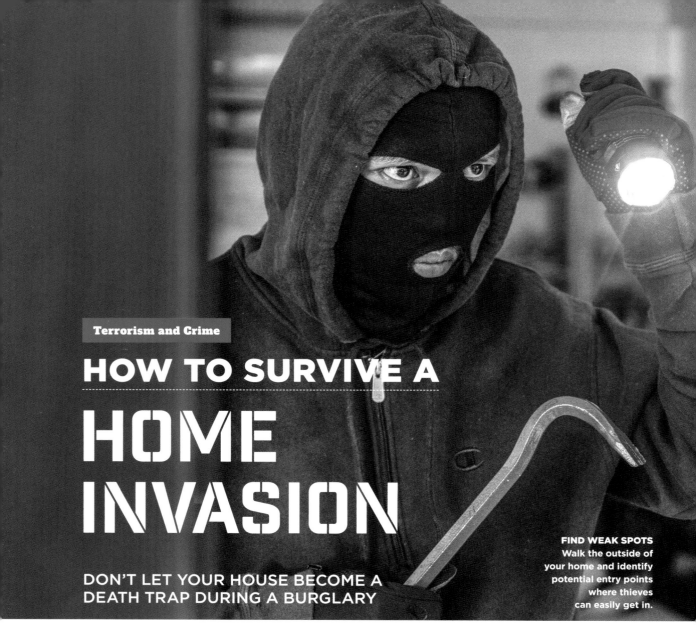

HOW TO SURVIVE A

HOME INVASION

DON'T LET YOUR HOUSE BECOME A DEATH TRAP DURING A BURGLARY

FIND WEAK SPOTS
Walk the outside of your home and identify potential entry points where thieves can easily get in.

> Of the approximately 3.7 million home break-ins each year in the United States, about 28 percent of them take place when somebody's home. The fear and violation are traumatic enough. But in about 7 percent of those cases, the resident gets assaulted. If you can't scare off a home invader, learn how to protect yourself and your family.

LET THEM KNOW YOU'RE AT HOME

Your average thief wants to hit an empty home and not tangle with a frightened, and possibly armed, resident. When you hear a knock at the front, yell, "I'll get it," so they know somebody's inside. If you hear rattling around outside, turn on lights and make lots of noise. Bang a pot or put the TV on full blast. Keep your remote car keys near you at night. If somebody is trying to break in, you can press the alarm button and scare them off.

BURGLAR-PROOF THE HOUSE

Plant shrubs with spikes and thorns near windows and doors. It will not only tear at the intruder's clothing and skin, but also collect blood that can later be tested for DNA. If you don't have a security system, put fake alarm stickers on the windows.

DESIGNATE A SAFE ROOM

Make a plan with the family so everybody goes into the same room, which should have a strong lock, a flashlight and a landline phone. Come up with a code word so everybody will know when to head to the safe room.

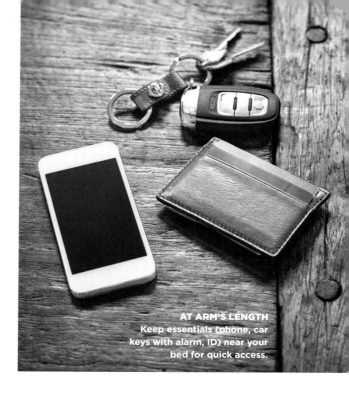

AT ARM'S LENGTH
Keep essentials (phone, car keys with alarm, ID) near your bed for quick access.

A FEW WORDS ABOUT GUNS

Whether or not you choose to keep a firearm in the house is a hot-button topic. If you do, be sure it's locked up, but in an accessible place in the safe room, next to a flashlight—and that you have been trained to use it properly.

Become a Good Knife-Fighter

You find an intruder in your house. You don't have a gun, but your kitchen is full of knives. Assuming you haven't completed thousands of hours of Navy SEAL training, here are several tips to maximize your chances of winning a knife fight.

1 SACRIFICIAL HAND Use your non-armed hand to fend off blows to the face, neck, stomach and chest.

2 GET A GRIP Grasp the knife hard and tight, like you're making a fist around the handle. Don't throw it, or you'll find yourself weaponless.

3 MOVE Dodge and weave while you wait for the perfect opportunity to attack. Give yourself space, preferably with room to back up.

4 TARGETS Go where they may not be expecting it: the femoral artery on each inner thigh. Otherwise, slash and stab the assailant on angles from his head down to his knees.

HOW TO SURVIVE

CYBER-TERRORISM

FROM LAPTOPS TO GOVERNMENT NETWORKS, THE RISK IS EVERYWHERE

> Cyberterrorism can include everything from hacking into a country's defense department computers to infecting people's PCs with viruses. It can be Russia posting fake news on Facebook. It can be hostile forces getting into a nuclear reactor's computer system. It's unpredictable and unaccountable. While the threat is global, the solution starts with you.

PROTECT WITH PASSWORDS

The fight against cyberattacks starts at your keyboard. Strengthen passwords to thwart entry into individual computers or entire systems. Use different passwords for different accounts, with a combination of capital and lowercase letters, numbers and symbols. Make the password at least eight characters long and hide it somewhere not easily found. Hint: Don't put it on a Post-it on your laptop.

EDUCATE YOURSELF

Many businesses, government departments and other organizations need to increase training for preventing cyber-intrusions and responding to them when they happen. Experts also call for more transparency with the public about recent cyberattacks. Along with password protection, people should be better informed about the techniques hackers use and simple ways to keep them away.

SHARED COMMUNICATION

With so many networks linked directly or indirectly, coordination between agencies and departments is vital. The FBI and Homeland Security have started working with local law enforcement agencies on a plan to respond to a cyberattack and share information about the latest technology and procedures. Such efforts are also expanding to businesses.

DON'T OVERREACT

A growing chorus of experts is cautioning against taking the fight too far and urging people not to conflate cybersecurity with cyberterrorism. Yes, the incursions have cost time and money and led to fear and worry. But so far, nobody has been physically harmed or killed in a cyberattack. Pipe bombs and rental trucks have caused much more havoc. Critics say knee-jerk responses could create unwarranted fear, fan discrimination and impinge on people's privacy rights.

PERSONAL SAFETY
Installing firewalls and virus-detection software on your home computer can help protect you from attacks.

79

HOW TO SURVIVE

ANTHRAX EXPOSURE

A POST-9/11 THREAT MADE CHECKING THE MAIL AN EXERCISE IN TERROR

> A week after the 9/11 terrorist attacks in 2001, letters laced with anthrax started arriving at media outlets and the offices of two U.S. senators. Five people died and more than a dozen others were infected. Dubbed Amerithrax, these incidents heightened fear of biological warfare. But they also spurred governments and health-care workers to better prepare.

SOS 101

A person with inhalation anthrax cannot transfer the disease to someone else. It can only be contracted by directly inhaling anthrax spores. So there is no need to worry about catching the disease from anyone else.

FINDING THE TRUTH
A special Amerithrax Task
Force completed more than
10,000 interviews in
the aftermath of the 2001
anthrax attacks.

IF YOU GET SUSPICIOUS MAIL

Don't shake the package or envelope or sniff, touch or taste any of the contents that spill out. Put it on the floor and leave the room, closing the door, then wash your hands with soap and water. Then alert the authorities.

GET TESTED QUICKLY

Inhalation of anthrax spores used to be a death sentence. But now, victims can survive if they get swift treatment from antibiotics and antitoxins. Two Amerithrax victims who were treated within three days of the appearance of symptoms lived. But two victims who were treated five to seven days later died.

RECOGNIZE THE SYMPTOMS

Anthrax symptoms look very much like those of other common ailments: runny nose, chills, fever, fatigue and nausea. Because speedy treatment is of the essence, correct diagnosis is critical.

81

CHAPTER 03

OUT IN THE WILD

> It's a jungle out there, even if you're swimming in the ocean, where every week is Shark Week. When you venture into the great outdoors, you're living by wildlife rules, not yours. Discover what makes bears, mountain lions, alligators, sharks, snakes and mosquitoes bite and stingrays sting—and what you can do about it.

SAFE SPACE
With simple precautions,
you'll find the ocean is big
enough for both of you.

HOW TO SURVIVE A

DEADLY SHARK

FREE YOURSELF FROM THOSE POWERFUL JAWS BY FIGHTING BACK

> The good news is you'll probably never get eaten by a shark. Despite the hype from *Jaws* and the Discovery Channel's Shark Week, the chances you'll be killed by this fish (yes, it is a fish!) are one in 3.8 million, according to the International Shark Attack File. The bad news is that shark attacks are on the rise. Climate change not only has the creatures heading farther north due to warmer waters, it also has more people swimming in the ocean—a deadly combination. If you do get attacked by a shark, the best strategy is to play by the fish's rules, not yours.

AVOID DANGEROUS WATERS

Out of more than 375 shark species, only a dozen are dangerous, and just three are responsible for most human attacks: great white, tiger and bull sharks. Humans are not, however, their preferred food source. To avoid an attack, steer clear of river mouths and harbor entrances, and don't swim early in the morning or late at night. Also stay away from fishing boats tossing chum and dead fish into the water, since the blood attracts sharks.

BE ALERT

Swim with buddies and stay aware of your surroundings. If you're shipwrecked or fall overboard and don't have goggles, improvise. According to Shark Week host Terry Schappert: "Our eyes don't focus in water; they focus in air. If I look through [a water bottle], I can actually see all around me. I can cover all sorts of angles, including directly below me—because when sharks come, they come silently."

STAY CALM

That shark with a hungry look might just be checking you out, like a curious puppy… albeit one with several rows of razor-sharp teeth. Don't provoke it by splashing and kicking. Think of the shark as an unwanted visitor in a singles bar; give it the stink-eye. Like humans, this makes them uncomfortable and they might go away. At worst they may take a few nips, realize you're not lunch, then move on. Granted, these "love bites" could still require extensive surgery and months of recovery, but they won't kill you. "A shark has got no paws or hands, so if it wants to explore something, the only way it can do that is to put it in its mouth," said Richard Peirce, former chairman of the U.K.-based Shark Trust charity. "That's why we often get exploratory bites that don't result in death and sometimes don't even result in serious injury."

SHOW HIM WHO'S BOSS

If none of this works and the shark attacks anyway, then it's time to put up a fight. "You want to be aggressive, because sharks appreciate size and power," advised George Burgess, curator of the International Shark Attack File (ISAF) at the Florida Museum of Natural History. "You want to fight like hell. Demonstrate you're strong and not going to go down easy." Go for one of the shark's most sensitive areas. "Hit it on the nose hard," Burgess told *Time*. "It will probably be surprised and won't know what's going on for a moment or two." Or smack it in the eyes, like surfer Scott Stephens did when a 10-foot great white shark took a bite out of his side in 2012 in Eureka, California. "I was able to torque my body and punch it behind its right eye," he told *Outside* magazine. "It immediately let me go and swam down and toward shore."

SEEK HELP

Needless to say, if the shark bites you, get medical assistance as quickly as possible. A shark attack does not have to be fatal. Shark teeth are very sharp, like scalpels, and can leave clean wounds that can be easily sewn up. Get to shore, apply pressure to stop blood loss, and in the case of a lost limb, apply a tourniquet (see page 87).

I Survived...
A SHARK ATTACK

Amonth after a shark tore off her left arm in waters off Kauai, Hawaii, in 2003, 13-year-old Bethany Hamilton vowed to get back on her board and pursue her dream of becoming a professional surfer.

Her life had been saved by a family friend who used a surfboard leash as a tourniquet to stop the bleeding. Hamilton recovered fast enough to return to the water within weeks, teaching herself how to surf with one arm by putting more force into her kicks. She went on to score eight first-place finishes in competitions around the world.

Her 2004 autobiography, *Soul Surfer: A True Story of Faith, Family, and Fighting to Get Back on Board*, hit the big screen as a feature film, and *Unstoppable*, a documentary about her life, was released in 2018.

Now a married mom juggling family life and pro surfing, Hamilton told *The Guardian* in 2016, "It's almost like my surfing has been overshadowed by being a shark-attack survivor and being known as Soul Surfer." Still, she acknowledges that's a good problem to have.

"I'm thankful to be alive!" Hamilton wrote on Instagram on the 14th anniversary of the October 31st shark attack. "I look back and would not change that day otherwise. God can truly turn pain into beauty. We can grow through our hard times and overcome. Happy stumpy day to me."

Stop Massive Bleeding From a Shark Attack

Even when a shark takes out a big chunk of a swimmer's limb, victims have been able to survive. First aid delivered quickly and properly can stop the bleeding until help arrives, but may take improvisation. Have someone else call 911 while you tend to the victim, so precious time is not wasted.

1 ACCESS THE WOUND Cut away the victim's wet suit (if wearing one) to get a clear look at the injury, then apply direct pressure on the wound with sterile gauze, if you have it, or a beach towel or T-shirt if you don't. Pressure is only a temporary measure to buy time for the next steps.

2 ATTACH THE TOURNIQUET AND STICK Wrap a surf leash around the wound 2 inches toward the body, away from the wound or a joint. Knot the leash on top, then attach a stick (for torsion) with two more knots.

3 TWIST Turn the stick to tighten the leash around the limb until the bleeding stops. Tie the stick to the limb with another knot. If the victim screams out, this is to be expected. Done right, a tourniquet should hurt.

4 WATCH FOR SHOCK. Symptoms include cold or blue skin, fast breathing and confusion. Place the victim on his back and put a blanket over him.

MOUTH OFF
Alligators can weigh over
1,000 pounds and have
a powerful bite, but the
muscles that open their
jaws are relatively weak.

HOW TO SURVIVE AN

ANGRY ALLIGATOR

RUN AWAY IN A STRAIGHT LINE AS FAST AS YOU CAN—OR BE PREPARED TO FIGHT LIKE HELL

On a night in June of 2016, a 2-year-old boy named Lane Graves was playing on the shores of Disney World's Seven Seas Lagoon in Orlando, Florida, when he was snapped up by a lunging alligator that dragged him underwater. Lane was found dead the next day. With an estimated 1.3 million gators, Florida has long tangled with the ancient reptiles as development encroaches upon their habitats. Only about a dozen bites a year are recorded and few are fatal, with only 24 since records began in 1948. But it does happen. Here's how to avoid becoming a statistic.

⚠DANGER

ALLIGATORS AND SNAKES IN AREA

STAY AWAY FROM THE WATER

DO NOT FEED THE WILDLIFE

LOVE FOR LANE CELEBRATION Friends and family gathered on September 3, 2016, to commemorate what would have been Lane's 3rd birthday.

DON'T BE EASY PREY

Don't try to feed alligators, or even approach them. In fact, feeding them is against Florida law; it just makes them less afraid of humans. Avoid swimming in fresh water during peak alligator activity time—between dusk and dawn. And always watch out for children, who, to an alligator, closely resemble their usual diet of small mammals. Be extra careful during the summer mating season, when all that egg-laying has the alligators extra hungry.

RUN LIKE HELL

If an alligator starts approaching, get out of the water. Then run like your life depends on it, because it does. Alligators can lunge quickly (at speeds of more than 20 mph)—but most humans can outrun them, leaving the gator to slink back into the water, hunting for easier prey. Remember, they're alligators, not snipers, so run in a straight line, not a zigzag.

You want to get out of their territory as fast as possible. A safe distance, according to experts, is 20 to 30 feet away.

MAKE A COMMOTION

If you can't get away, put up a fight. According to the Florida Fish and Wildlife Conservation Commission, "The best thing you can do is fight back, making as much noise and commotion as possible, hitting or kicking the alligator." If you observe an alligator attack, scream and clap. The gator might decide this meal isn't worth the effort.

HIT 'EM WHERE IT HURTS

They may be covered in natural armor, but alligators have vulnerable spots. While it might be difficult to manage during the throes of an attack, aiming for the snout or poking the eyes may irritate the gator enough to get it to release you from its jaws.

I Survived...
AN ALLIGATOR ATTACK

On May 7, 2017, 10-year-old Juliana Ossa was splashing around in 2 feet of water in a lake in Orlando, Florida, when an alligator bit her on the left leg.

"I tried hitting it on the forehead to let me go," the girl told the *Today* show. "That didn't work, so I thought of a plan they taught at [Orlando alligator zoo] Gatorland. The guy was wrestling the alligator with its mouth taped, and in this situation it was the other way around. So I stuck my two fingers up its nose so it couldn't breathe—it had to [breathe] from its mouth, and he opened it, so it let my leg out." Juliana's step-uncle Steven Rodriguez pulled her to shore and she was rushed to the hospital, where she was treated for lacerations and puncture wounds to her leg. "Ten years old, to do what she did—to have that much wherewithal to do what she did—that is incredible," Tim Williams of Gatorland told *Inside Edition*. "We are so proud of her that she was able to get out of there with as little damage as she got."

HOW TO SURVIVE A

FEROCIOUS BEAR

KNOW WHO YOU'RE DEALING WITH

In September 2019, four hunters were injured in three separate attacks by grizzly bears in Montana's Gravelly mountains. Though all survived, and bear attacks in the U.S. are rare—there are only about 11 each year—they can happen. It pays to be prepared if you're in a region—mostly the Northern and Western U.S.—where bears are common. Black bears are usually less aggressive and more tolerant of people than grizzlies (also called brown bears), and they're more likely to live nearer to humans. When feeling threatened, black bears may run to climb a tree. Grizzly bears, on the other hand, stay away from densely populated areas. They don't climb as well, though, and may turn and attack—especially if they get surprised. If you happen upon a bear who looks like he might charge, here's what you can do.

WALK DON'T RUN

Bears can charge at speeds up to 35 miles per hour from a dead stop, so it's unlikely you could outrun one. But if you happen upon a bear that is minding its own business, it's best to back away slowly until you're out of its line of sight. If you're worried about surprising a bear in its territory, bringing a dog with you or making noise by clapping or calling out as you hike can alert them so they move away. They don't want to see you in most cases, either. If you do see one, leave the area immediately.

SPRAY AWAY

A mother bear is super-protective of her cubs and will likely view you as a threat—never get between a mama and her babies. If you've been making noise and still happen upon a bear, it's wise to be carrying a whistle and bear spray (similar to pepper spray), and to have trained ahead in how to use it. The spray has been shown to be better at deterring attacks than guns; however, it only works if the bear is 40 feet or closer. It may help fend off a curious bear, but against a charging grizzly it's not going to be of much use. Flares, especially marine flares that put out a lot of noise and light, can sometimes work to scare off a curious bear as well—although you don't want to start a forest fire, so training is useful for them as well.

GET LARGE

Same as with a dog attack, if a bear is charging you, make yourself as big as possible. A grizzly bear can stand up to 8 feet tall on its hind legs, but if you wave your arms and make noise, he'll see you as a somewhat equal opponent and may back down. If you have a rifle, aim at a spot below the bear's chin or just behind its front legs if you're shooting at it from the side.

STAND STILL OR PLAY DEAD

If you are unarmed, you might stand totally still. Bears have been known to false-charge to test their opponent. Or, as retired Navy SEAL Clint Emerson explains, you can also play dead. In *100 Deadly Skills: Survival Edition*, he says playing dead is successful 75 percent of the time. "Lie flat on your stomach to protect your organs, crossing your hands behind your neck to guard your arteries," he suggests. "Or curl into the fetal position." If the bear thinks you're no longer a threat, it may lose interest.

FIGHT! FIGHT! FIGHT!

If you are an unlucky victim of the very rare predatory attack, in which a bear intends to kill and eat you for dinner, fight back however you can with whatever weapons you have at your disposal: your fists, rocks, sticks, a knife. Aim for the eyes and nose, where the bear is sensitive. A grizzly bear's bite holds 1,200 pounds per square inch of force, so there's no question that you are in a fight to the death, but with these tips, you may be better prepared to come out of it alive.

ROOM TO ROAM
A grizzly's home range can stretch up to 600 square miles.

HOW TO SURVIVE

POUNCING MOUNTAIN LION

THERE ARE MORE MEET-UPS THAN EVER

With human populations encroaching on lions' natural habitats (hillsides and mountain terrain), there's been an increase in encounters in recent years. Yet according to the California Department of Fish and Wildlife (CDFW), only three of their 18 verified mountain lion attacks since 1986 ended in a fatality. Here's how to stay safe.

TAKE EVERY PRECAUTION

If your home is near mountain lion country, remove any dense vegetation from around your house and install ample outdoor lighting; both will help you be able to spot any approaching danger.

STAY ALERT

Cougars are most active at dawn, dusk and at night, so try not to be in their habitat at those times. Stay extra vigilant if you are, especially if you have an unleashed dog with you.

STAND TALL, BUT STILL

Maintain eye contact and never put your back to the cat. Try to look as big as possible and slowly wave your arms above your head. (And pick up any children that are with you.)

USE YOUR OUTDOOR VOICE

Speak slowly but loudly to disrupt the animal's hunting instincts. Don't screech or yell at a high pitch—it can make you sound like prey.

GIVE IT ALL YOU'VE GOT

If you're attacked, fight back with any weapon you can: a walking stick, a knife, rocks, a jacket, even your own hand. Aim to strike the cat in its head and eyes, which can confuse it.

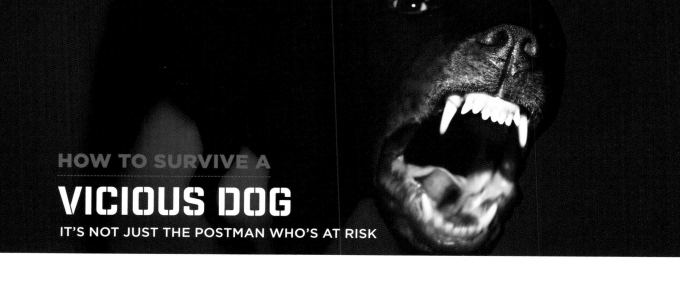

HOW TO SURVIVE A
VICIOUS DOG
IT'S NOT JUST THE POSTMAN WHO'S AT RISK

They are affectionately known as "man's best friend," but not all dogs are equally cuddly. There's a reason police departments and the military train canines for dangerous work, like chasing down predators—dogs can be trained to be ruthless and dangerous. But even household pets can sometimes act out, resulting in a bite. Of the approximately 4.5 million dog bites that occur each year, one in five becomes infected, so knowing what to do if you do get bit is key.

RESPECT THE ROTTWEILER
The easiest way to deal with a bite is to not get one in the first place. Any pooch can be dangerous, so it's best not to tease them, even if they look harmless—especially if a dog is chained, which could lead it to be aggressive. If a dog is baring its teeth, growling or otherwise shows signs of hyper-alertness, respect its space and give it a wide berth. If there's no way to avoid the dog, make yourself less of a threat by standing sideways, don't run and don't smile! A dog can read that as you baring your teeth. Back away carefully and slowly.

SHOW YOUR BARK
If a dog continues to approach in attack mode, you still should not run, as the dog will chase. But if you can find a way to get up high, in a tree or on a fence, that might take you out of harm's way, because dogs can't climb. If that isn't an option, make like a big dog and raise your arms above your head to make yourself seem larger than you are and roar loudly. If there's anything to throw at the dog, like stones, that may deter it.

RUN INTERFERENCE
If the dog is nearly on top of you, you may be able to avoid being bitten by putting something in his way that he can bite instead, like a jacket or backpack. If you have time to wrap a jacket or sweater around your arm to offer the dog, that can result in less bleeding and you'll still have three limbs to fight with. Surprisingly, a firearm is only 80 percent effective in stopping a charging pit bull according to animals24-7.org. But other heavy objects, like a fire extinguisher, can do the trick. As can a bite stick—something thick enough, like a baseball bat, that the dog can latch onto.

REDUCE THE SEVERITY OF THE BITE
You can throw yourself on the dog and try to crack its ribs, which are easily broken. Or push against the bite, which can force a dog to open its mouth. If that doesn't work, go for the dog's eyes or try to strike it at the back of the head at the base of the skull. Pit bulls aren't deterred by pain, however, so be warned.

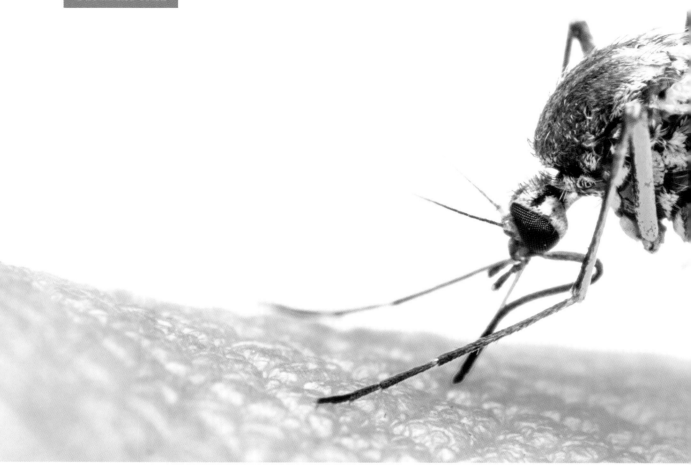

HOW TO SURVIVE A

LETHAL MOSQUITO

PROTECT YOURSELF FROM THE MOST DANGEROUS INSECT IN THE WORLD

So tiny you can squash it with your pinkie, yet so deadly it can kill millions, the mosquito is the world's deadliest insect. Carrying diseases including the West Nile virus, dengue fever and chikungunya, this pest infects the bloodstream through its bite. The most serious mosquito-borne disease is malaria, killing 1 million people a year, many of them children. The Zika virus, which is carried by mosquitoes and was spread through the Americas in the mid-2010s, was declared a global public health emergency in 2016, since there is no vaccine or treatment.

Yet taking some simple precautions can ward off many mosquito risks.

HOME IMPROVEMENTS
Drain areas of standing water in your yard (that's where mosquitoes spawn), and install screens over windows. Use fans to keep air circulating—mosquitoes hate breezes.

COVER UP
Since mosquitoes are attracted to dark colors, wear white or tan clothing, and cover as much of the skin as possible with long-sleeved shirts and long pants.

USE BUG SPRAY
"Using an insect repellent is one of the best ways you can protect yourself from Zika and other diseases transmitted by mosquitoes," said Harry Savage, chief of ecology and entomology activity at the CDC's Division of Vector-Borne Diseases. *Consumer Reports* has found repellents that work best contain 15 to 30 percent DEET, 20 percent picaridin or 30 percent OLE (oil of lemon eucalyptus), giving their highest ranking to CVS brand Total Home. They also noted that products made with natural plant oils, such as citronella and lemongrass oil, were not effective.

FAST FACT

Snakes have flexible jaws that allow them to eat prey bigger than their head.

HOW TO SURVIVE A
KILLER SNAKE
SERPENTS BECOME MORE DANGEROUS AS THEIR HABITAT EXPANDS

Snakebites kill more than 90,000 people a year worldwide, with 7,000 to 8,000 victims of venomous bites in the United States. It's not that snakes have become more aggressive. "The numbers are going up… because as we have more global warming, the snakes can do better further north," explains Dr. Joann Schulte, an epidemiologist with the North Texas Poison Control Center.

AN OUNCE OF PREVENTION...

While the number of snakes—and snake bites—is on the rise, there are things you can do to protect yourself from the fanged creatures. When you are out in areas where snakes tend to be, like near water and in forests, wear closed shoes. Stick to a path, avoid areas of overgrown vegetation and don't tread lightly. Since snakes don't hear very well, you'll want to make vibrations to let them know you're coming. They want nothing to do with you, either. But if you sneak up on them, they might attack in self-defense.

BEWARE THE DEAD

Whatever you do, don't pick up a dead snake. "Snakes are well-known for retaining reflexes after death," said Steven Beaupre, a biology professor at the University of Arkansas. In fact, thanks to reflexes in their brains, a venomous snake like a cobra or a rattlesnake can bite even hours after its death. A Washington State man found out the hard way when he decapitated a rattlesnake with a shovel and was bitten when he picked up its remains.

IF YOU GET BIT

Get to a hospital ASAP, says Lori Weichenthal, a wilderness-medicine expert at the University of California-San Francisco. Immobilize the bitten limb and keep it below heart level. Don't waste your money on a snake-bite kit—they don't often work, and may do more harm than good. Home remedies, like trying to suck the venom out or taking a shot of alcohol, are ineffective. Antivenin at the hospital is your best bet.

While sharks get the most attention, they're not the only deadly animals beneath the surface. These gentle swimmers turn angry—fast—when provoked or stressed.

PIRANHA

These Amazonian river fish usually only attack humans when stressed during the dry season, when the waters are low and food is scarce. Avoid splashing, which draws their attention, and get out of the water if you're bleeding, since blood attracts them. Most wounds are easily treated bites to feet and ankles.

LARGE SEA WASP

It floats like a ghost and stings with the most powerful venom of any animal on Earth. The box jellyfish, also called the sea wasp, packs enough venom to kill 60 adults. If you don't drown or suffer a heart attack from the intense pain, remove the tentacles with a towel or while wearing gloves and wash the area with vinegar. Ice cubes can dull the pain. Then get to the hospital.

BLUE RINGED OCTOPUS

When angry, this pale little 8-inch-long octopus—which lives in tidal pools and coral reefs from Japan to Australia—turns bright yellow, and its 50-plus rings flash bright blue. The bite is painless, but the venom can leave victims paralyzed but awake, unable to breath or call for help. Apply pressure to the wound, perform mouth-to-mouth resuscitation, and hope the victim recovers, because there's no antivenin.

STINGRAY

The barbed tail is generally only fatal when it punctures a vital area of the body. You will likely need to have a doctor remove the stinger. Victims will need pain medication and a tetanus shot.

HOW TO SURVIVE A

SCARY
SEA
CREATURE

WATCH WHERE YOU WADE.
THESE GUYS ALSO PACK A
NASTY BITE AND STING

FACING THE ELEMENTS

> Whether you're lost in the jungle, stranded on a deserted island or off course when hiking in the mountains, keeping your wits about you and taking some basic preparative measures can help boost your odds of survival when you're away from civilization.

DON'T GO IT ALONE
Stay with your vehicle if it breaks down—it's easier for rescuers to detect a car or truck from the air than it is to find a human being wandering out in the open.

HOW TO SURVIVE IN THE

DESERT

VAST, DRY, HOT AND FORBIDDING, THE DESOLATE WASTELAND POSES THE ULTIMATE CHALLENGE

> The unrelenting sun beats down and your mind starts playing tricks on you. Is that water up ahead? Or is it just a mirage? Few things can be more terrifying than getting lost in the desert. Every move you make counts in preserving every ounce of precious water.

ON THE ATTACK
Scorpions are patient hunters and can spend hours in one spot, waiting for a victim to come close enough to strike.

RATION YOUR WATER

Just sitting in 90-degree temperatures for a few hours causes the body to lose at least six quarts of water. And that's in the shade. As deserts hit triple-digit temperatures, keeping hydrated becomes the No. 1 survival priority. No matter how hungry you get, avoid food—it only makes you thirstier. You can survive for days without food. You can't survive without water.

TRY AND FIND H20

Let nature lead you to water sources. Pigeons, doves and bees all stay close to water spots. Dig a few feet under a dry riverbed and you may find water, particularly if grasses or bushes are growing nearby. If you spot a glimmer amid some green, that could be a tinaja, or "earthen jar," a rocky depression with water.

BE NOCTURNAL

Find or build shelter and remain still during the day. Layer the ground with anything you can find; the ground could be 30 degrees hotter than the air. Keep your mouth closed and wrap your face with a bandanna, if you can. Limit your exertion to signaling for help with a mirror (if you have one) or any other piece of glass or shiny metal directed at the horizon. Only venture out in the evening and night. This can extend your survival period from hours to days.

LOOK FOR CREEPY CRAWLIES

The desert is crawling with spiders and scorpions that may find their way into your shoes or sleeping bag. A rattlesnake could lurk behind that next rock. Check your shoes and socks before putting them on, and watch your step.

STAY IN THE CAR

If you are driving and break down in the middle of nowhere, resist the urge to set out for help. Your car will be the best shelter you can find. If you do think you see a house or business or source of water close enough to hike toward, leave a note in the car to say which direction you're going. That oasis of help may turn out to be a mirage.

GOOD SIGN
The flight path of birds may lead you to water.

FAST FACT

Mirages are optical illusions that are caused by the refraction of light from the sky by heated air.

LAYER UP
Bring enough clothing to handle varying weather conditions.

HOW TO SURVIVE ON A
MOUNTAIN

UP WHERE THE AIR IS THIN, THE RISKS ARRIVE WHEN YOU LEAST EXPECT THEM

> In 2017, a Taiwanese couple wandered off a trail while trekking in the mountains of Nepal. They fell into a ravine, where they were stranded for seven weeks. While Liu Chen Chu (age 19) eventually died, her boyfriend, Liang Sheng Yueh (21) survived in time to be reached by rescuers, drinking melted snow and eating salt leftover from food. Here's how to avoid their fate.

INTO THE WILD
Don't bug
the wolves and
they should
leave you alone.

MAKE AN ITINERARY

Before you set out, write a detailed description of where you're going and when you expect to return, and leave it with a friend or family member. It will not only help them find you, it may help you spot potential problems in your plan.

AVOID HYPOTHERMIA

Even in summer, temperatures can drop to near freezing at night in the North American mountains. Rain or snow can hit with little warning. Keeping your body warm will be your first challenge.

SEEK PROTECTION

Locate shelter in a cave or protected area that still affords you a good view of rescuers.

Using branches and leaves, build a lean-to that doesn't face the wind, and cover the ground with additional leaves.

BUILD A FIRE

Pile up firewood so you don't have to go searching for it in the middle of the night, and build a fire surrounded by rocks, which will absorb, store and radiate heat. The fire will not only keep you warm, but it can be used to purify water from streams and send up smoke as a signal for help.

ROUTE TO SAFETY

Your best option is usually to stay put and wait for help. But if you have to go, follow rivers downstream, as most settlements are built next to water, and you'll be able to find help.

Purifying Water Essentials

Since the human body can only go three days without water, getting it is critical. Most spring water, new snow, dew and rain that hasn't fallen through forest canopies should be safe. Water from streams, rivers and lakes needs to be purified. If you don't happen to have any of the many commercial filter products available, you'll have to boil it.

1 STRAIN Get out bugs, leaves, twigs and pebbles by running the water through a strainer. If you don't have cheesecloth handy, use a T-shirt or towel.

2 BOIL Ten minutes of a roiling boil will kill bacteria, viruses and parasites. If you don't have a fireproof container, put fire-heated rocks in the water. Boiling will not clean out everything— chemicals and heavy metals will remain—but it will clean the water enough to buy you time to get to safety or await rescue.

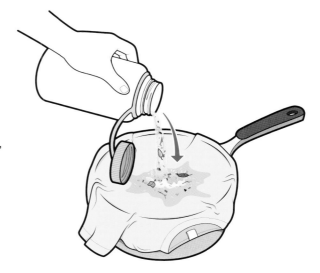

LIGHT IT UP
A fire or a flare can help you signal for help from passing ships, planes or other rescue operations.

HOW TO SURVIVE ON A

DESERTED ISLAND

TAKE SOME TIPS OUT OF *ROBINSON CRUSOE* FOR FINDING FOOD, WATER AND SHELTER

> In the movie *Castaway*, Tom Hanks plays a FedEx executive who is stranded on a deserted island when his plane crashes over the Pacific Ocean. He survives for years thanks to his wits, his ingenuity, and a volleyball named Wilson for companionship. Staying alive in paradise takes ingenuity, hard work and a clear mindset.

DON'T PANIC
Those first few hours will send your emotions reeling. Take a moment to get your bearings and take stock. Where are you? Are you hurt? Are there others nearby? If so, find them. It's much easier to survive if tasks are delegated. Try to stay positive.

AVOID INJURY
Examine your body for cuts and scrapes; clean and bandage them as soon as possible. Small injuries can become big ones in the tropics, what with gangrene and other problems. If you're not fit, you're of little value to yourself and others.

SCAVENGE FOR SUPPLIES
Before high tide or rains arrive, look for things that may have washed up with you that will be helpful. Water bottles and food cans are the highest priority. Also look for tools. Anything that cuts is vital. So are hammers and pliers. Plastic sheeting can be used for shelter. Even garbage is of value—a sharp piece of metal would make a very nice spear for fishing or fending off animals.

BUILD A SHELTER
Wind, sun and rain will quickly take their toll. Evening thunderstorms are common on desert islands, so you could end up chilled to the bone and suffering from hypothermia. Find a cave or make a lean-to. Cover the ground and try not to sleep directly on it.

MAKE A FIRE
Binoculars and glasses can pinpoint sunlight onto a leaf. You can also make a fire with sticks and a board. It'll take some time, but it will be worth it. A fire will also help you avoid coming into contact with bugs and snakes, which may be poisonous.

OBTAIN A SOURCE OF WATER
The body can only go a few days without water. Find sources of non-salt water. Springs, rivers, dew and captured rainwater are probably safe. Boil all other water for 10 minutes. Even pristine-looking streams can contain parasites and bacteria.

FIND FOOD
Small fish in shallow waters are your best bet, as are mollusks (oysters, clams and mussels). Seaweed that's growing, not washed up, can also be a good source of nutrients. Cook everything to rid it of bacteria or parasites. To determine if a food is poisonous, rub a little on the back of your hand to see if you get a reaction. If not, carefully place a little on your tongue, then wait.

CREATE A RESCUE SIGNAL
Rescuers will be looking for you, so let them know where you are. That fire will be your best signal. Put some damp moss or wet logs on it to increase smoke. Write "SOS" in the sand and fill it with stones so it'll stand out. Stay put and wait for help.

GO INSIDE
The farther inland you go on a desert island, the better your chance of finding fresh water.

Start a Fire

It doesn't get any more basic than this. Rub a stick onto a board to create enough friction heat to ignite tinder. The secret is to press down hard while rubbing fast.

1 FIND A STICK Round off one end of a softwood (pine or fir) stick.

2 GET FIREBOARD Cut a hole in a wood board about an inch from the edge. Then cut a V-shaped notch connecting the edge of the board to the hole, with the point of the V against the hole.

3 USE TINDER Put dry tinder in the V notch.

4 DRILL, BABY, DRILL Place the stick into the hole and rub it back and forth with your palms while pressing down until the friction causes heat and smoke.

5 BLOW GENTLY Blow onto the smoldering tinder to make it flame.

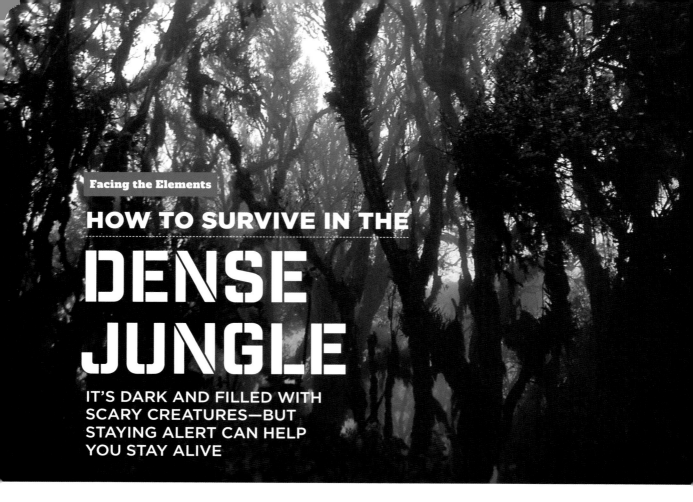

HOW TO SURVIVE IN THE

DENSE JUNGLE

IT'S DARK AND FILLED WITH SCARY CREATURES—BUT STAYING ALERT CAN HELP YOU STAY ALIVE

In 2019, yoga teacher Amanda Eller made national news after getting lost in a Hawaiian jungle for 17 days and living to tell about it, despite suffering a fall and a broken leg. Her greatest survival tool? Her mind. "There were times of total fear and loss and I wanted to give up, and it did come down to life and death. I chose life," Eller revealed after her miraculous rescue. Beyond sheer determination, these practical skills will also serve you well.

STAY HYDRATED

Look for large leaves that can collect rainfall to divert it directly into your mouth or into any bottle you might have. Freshly caught rain from natural pools in rock formations is the next-best option; they're less likely to be contaminated than other sources. Water from streams should be boiled (in a pot, a single-walled stainless steel water bottle or metal container) over a fire to kill any bacteria. See "Collecting Water," right, for how to build a solar water sill, another helpful option.

MONKEY SEE, MONKEY DO

Since a lot of vegetation isn't safe to eat, one trick is to observe monkeys in the area to

LUCKY LADY
Amanda Eller survived more than two weeks in the Hawaiian jungle.

see what fruits and plants they're munching. Beyond that, stick with foods you recognize and know to be edible (bananas, avocados, oranges, etc.). A few general guidelines on anything unfamiliar to you: Avoid mushrooms (most will be poisonous); skip anything with thorns or shiny leaves; pass on plants that have white or yellow berries; if something has a bitter or soapy taste, spit it out immediately.

A MIND FOR MEAT

Trapping an animal will be easier than hunting for one, unless you're a seasoned, skilled hunter. To trap, dig a hole (make it deep enough so if an animal falls in, it can't climb out before you kill it) and cover it. Then place some fruit or other type of bait on top. Fishing will be easier. Fashion a four-pronged spear out of a bamboo stalk to fish in streams or knee-deep water.

LEAVE A TRAIL

To help any rescuers who might be looking for you, break branches at eye level as you travel so they know which way you were heading. Or make conspicuous rock piles to direct them.

TRAVEL WITH PURPOSE

You'll want to stay on the move as much as possible to get to safety, but be conscious of which direction you're traveling. Jungles can be disorienting, so to avoid wasting energy walking in circles, you'll need to identify one reference point in front of you and one

reference point behind you. Also, remember that streams or rivers will generally lead to civilization, so be on the lookout for those. Travel by the light of day to stay on the move, and rest up at night to prevent injuries that will make finding help that much harder.

ARM YOURSELF

If you're stranded without a knife, try to use a rock to fashion a sharp-edged spear out of a large stick or piece of bamboo. Keep that spear with you at all times, to protect yourself from wild animals.

HUNKER DOWN

For shelter, build something simple, but that will protect you from the elements. A lean-to will probably work best: Get one long stick and lean it against a tree. Then find smaller branches and layer them at 45-degree angles against either side of the large one. Cover the entire structure with leaves, which will also help you conserve your own heat.

COLLECTING WATER

HOW TO MAKE A SOLAR WATER SILL:

To collect potable, distilled water, start by digging a hole in the soil. Place a container of some sort in the middle of the hole, padding any gaps around the container with wet leaves. Then place a plastic sheet over the hole, anchoring the sheet with larger rocks around its edges. When done, place a small rock in the center of the plastic, just over the container. Condensation will eventually gather on the underside of the plastic and then run down its center, dripping into the container.

PLANES, TRAINS, AUTOMOBILES AND SHIPS

> No destination is worth some harrowing journeys. When the plane dives, the ship capsizes, the car catches on fire or the train hops the rails, survival could hinge on something as small as the seat you selected. With images of twisted metal and shattered glass, transportation disasters dominate the news. Get the untold story.

SURVIVOR SEARCH
Fifteen people were rescued alive from a Taipei river after this TransAsia crash that killed 31 in 2015.

HOW TO SURVIVE A

PLANE CRASH

WHERE YOU SIT AND WHEN YOU SLEEP COULD DETERMINE YOUR FATE

> When commercial airlines crash, the number of fatalities is often enormous. But flying is the safest form of mass transportation (you have only a one in 9,821 chance of dying in an air or space transport incident). The National Transportation Safety Board examined 568 commercial airline crashes in the United States between 1993 and 2000, involving 53,000 passengers and crew, and found that 90 percent of people onboard lived. In fact, most people who die in survivable crashes do so after the aircraft comes to a complete stop, because they are unprepared for the crash. Here, a few ways you can help yourself walk away.

TIMING IS EVERYTHING
The vast majority of crashes occur during the so-called "Plus 3/Minus 8" period: three minutes after takeoff and eight minutes before landing. These are the times to be most prepared. Don't nod off to sleep. By all means save those sleeping pills for later. If the plane does go down, most fatalities are caused by fire, not by the crash itself, so be ready to react quickly and evacuate. According to studies, you have 90 seconds to get out before flames engulf the plane.

CHOOSE A SAFER SEAT
Debate swirls around whether one seat location is safer than another. *Popular Mechanics* studied the issue and found: "Passengers [seated] near the tail of a plane are about 40 percent more likely to survive a crash than those in the first few rows up front." That's because the front rows are vulnerable to frontal impacts. Passengers seated within five rows of exits are also believed to have a better chance of survival.

BRACE YOURSELF
One of the first pieces of advice you'll hear when you board a plane is how to adopt the brace position. You have to put your feet and knees together, rest your feet firmly on the floor, wear your seat belt low and place your head against the surface of the seat in front. Doing this will result in less severe injuries because it will help keep your limbs from flailing and you won't hit your head on the front seat during impact. This means it's more likely you can escape the crashed plane without broken bones.

FLY BIGGER PLANES
According to safety studies, private jets are four times more dangerous than commercial airlines. Also, large airlines have better safety records than regional carriers.

HUMAN ERROR Poor flight planning and other mistakes were blamed for the 2016 crash in Colombia that killed 71.

In Loving Memory
Our family members and friends
Who lost their lives in
the tragic accident
of Ukraine Airlines flight crash

FAST FACT

People are less likely to survive a crash into a lake or ocean because of the risks of drowning and hypothermia.

MIRACLE ON THE HUDSON
A US Airways plane landed
safely on the water in New
York in 2009 thanks to the
quick thinking of Captain
Chesley "Sully" Sullenberger.

TERROR IN THE SKY
Despite massive damage, only one person died.

I Survived...
ALOHA FLIGHT 243

A passenger on Aloha Airlines Flight 243, Albert "Al" Ruhl watched a third of the plane's fuselage violently rip away midair on April 28, 1988. At 24,000 feet, 89 passengers and six crew members struggled to breathe and evade debris that had been turned into projectiles. Flight attendant Clarabelle Lansing, 58, was swept away, never to be found. Another flight attendant and seven passengers were seriously wounded and dozens more sustained minor injuries during the 13-minute ordeal, which was later blamed on poor maintenance and inspection procedures.

Stewardess Clarabelle Lansing greeted me at the boarding gate with a pretty smile and plumeria in her hair. The flight was leaving on schedule at 1:25 p.m., and I took my seat, 15C, near the wing flap, settling in for a short ride to Honolulu, where I was looking forward to surprising my wife, Elaine, with some of her favorite anthurium flowers.

Things were going pretty smoothly, the weather was nice, and beverage service was underway as we reached 24,000 feet. That's when a thunderous din was followed by a whoosh of air, and I was pulled forward despite my seat belt, crushing the tray table with my body.

The wind was unbelievable. The sound, deafening. It was difficult to breathe. The roof was tearing off from left to right, and a white mist and heavy debris flew through the freezing-cold cabin, creating a unique sort of blizzard.

One stewardess, Michelle Honda, was thrown, but she managed to wrap her right arm around the base of a seat across from me, and I grasped her left arm. When I looked up, I could see that Clarabelle, who had been serving drinks to first-class passengers, was gone. Sunshine poured through a hole the size of a door above where she had been standing. The remaining roof and walls around the hole crumpled and blew away.

Seeing an 18-foot stretch of exposed cabin, I thought it was all over, as did those around me, who were eerily silent after the initial screams. One couple hugged and said goodbye. I prayed, thanking God for a very good life. But it wasn't my time.

In the cockpit, the door had been torn off and Capt. Robert Schornstheimer said he could see blue sky where the first-class ceiling had been. He and First Officer Madeline Lynn Tompkins acted fast, declaring an emergency, coordinating with ground crews and maintaining what control they could while diverting to Kahului Airport.

Michelle removed a life jacket from under a seat. She held it up for us to see and showed us how to put it on, which we did, and we put our heads down, ready for a crash that never came.

Touchdown—despite the gaping fuselage and a debris-damaged engine—was inexplicably smooth. It took a few moments before one passenger started to applaud, then we all joined in, and you'd have thought we won the World Series.

Can a Non-Pilot Really Land a Jumbo Jet?

Since 9/11, cockpit doors have been designed to keep people out. So devising a way to get to the radio and controls will be the first challenge a civilian will face to get into the cockpit and steer the plane to safety (pilots believe civilians have a 1 percent chance of success doing so). But if you do make it into the cockpit, here's what you need to know about the dizzying array of buttons, levers, screens, switches and pedals.

1 RADIO If the pilots are lost in mid-flight with the autopilot operating, you have to figure out how to use the radio, which is not as easy as it sounds. The button for the headset radio is on the steering wheel next to the button to disengage the autopilot—so let's stay away from that, and try using the hand-held radio. It'll probably be on the wrong frequency, as pilots switch from one to another during the flight, but whatever. Just yell "Mayday," and hopefully somebody will get the idea.

2 FINAL DESCENT That autopilot doesn't do everything. If somebody answers the distress call and if they can find somebody

who knows how to fly your plane, that somebody will talk you through the first leg of landing, leading the plane down to 1,500 feet. This requires a lot of button pushing and dial-reading and number-inputting to keep the plane at the right altitude, speed and direction.

3 LANDING Many planes have auto-land functions. Many don't. Let's hope this one does. Even so, this function also isn't as "auto" as the name implies. You'll have to steady the plane's lateral movement with the pedals, work the wing flaps, keep the airspeed right, keep the nose up and activate the landing gear. You'll be dialing in numbers and working your hands and feet all at once. Pilots spend months learning and years mastering this. You've got a few minutes. The good news is that about three miles from the runway, if you're positioned right, auto-land lands the plane. If you don't have auto-land, then you'll have to throw on the brakes and activate the thrusters to stop the plane and hope it doesn't skid off the runway, which, we'll just point out now, is one of the leading causes of air disasters.

RUSH-HOUR HORROR
The Portland, Oregon-bound train derailed onto cars and trucks but no motorists were killed.

HOW TO SURVIVE A

TRAIN DERAILMENT

FIND THE RIGHT SEAT IN THE RIGHT CAR. KNOW WHERE TO STAND AND WHERE TO GET OUT

> On the morning of Monday, December 18, 2017, Amtrak passenger train 501 departed Seattle for its inaugural trip to Portland, Oregon on the new Cascades line. After traveling about 40 miles south, the train reached a curve in the tracks and suddenly hurtled off an overpass, throwing its passenger cars onto vehicles on busy Interstate 5. The derailment killed at least three people on the train and sent dozens to the hospital with injuries. Although rail travel is statistically the safest mode of transportation after flying, the crash served as a reminder that accidents still happen. And when they do, the results can be dramatic, though experts say passengers can maximize safety by where they sit and what they do during the trip.

SOS 101

Don't try to beat a train at a crossing. They move faster than they appear. It takes up to a minute for a train traveling at 55 mph to stop.

DRAFT AN ESCAPE PLAN

As you take your seat, make a mental note of the location of the closest exit and familiarize yourself with how to open the emergency windows. Also look for the alarms and intercoms so that you can alert the conductor in case you encounter trouble during the ride.

FIND AN AISLE SEAT

You will miss the view but you'll have a clearer path to evacuation and be farther away from broken windows. This seat also protects you more from a side collision, which is considered by safety experts to be more probable than the train getting hit from the front or the back by another train.

CHOOSE THE SAFEST CAR

Although the middle car is considered safest in a collision from the front or the rear, most train crashes are derailments. In that case, the safest car is at least one back from the center car. "It comes down to physics and inertia," CNN's safety analyst David Soucie said after an Amtrak derailment in Philadelphia that killed seven in 2015. "Statistically speaking, the second car from the end would probably be the safest place to sit."

DON'T HANG AROUND THE CAFÉ CAR

Although it's great to have a place to enjoy a bite, it's better to grab your food and go. The café car is one of the most dangerous places during a crash, with food, equipment and non-seated passengers flying. Lavatories also offer no refuge, with sharp, hard edges inside.

SIT FACING BACKWARD

It may make you queasy while reading or working on the laptop, but sitting in a back-facing seat protects you if the train comes to a sudden stop. It's how Soucie always sits. "If there's an impact or if there was a derailment, you're forced back into your seat,

ON EDGE
Broken rails and welds are the most common causes of train derailments in the U.S.

and thereby you would stay in that seat, as opposed to facing forward, where you can become a projectile," he explained. Trains are not equipped with seat belts, like airplanes. Studies have shown that with the way the seats are designed, it's safer without belts, though every train derailment resurrects the debate about whether they should be installed.

HOW TO START YOUR EVACUATION

A derailment will wreak havoc inside the train, with bodies and belongings flying, glass breaking and people panicking. The car likely will be plunged into darkness and filled with smoke from fires. After an accident, get out of the train immediately. "It's going to be chaotic. You want to get on the floor. This is where you can breathe," Scott Sauer, an official with the Southeastern Pennsylvania Transportation Authority, told NBC News, demonstrating an evacuation by crawling down the aisle. "We have glow-in-the-dark

striping on the floor that's going to take you where you need to go, where your exit is."

OPEN A DOOR OR WINDOW

Manually open one of the big doors by pulling a red lever located to the side of the door behind a panel. To open emergency windows, yank on a rubber ring and pull the gasket off all the way around the window. The window will be heavy but it should pop out. If the car is upright, don't forget that it's a drop of eight feet or more to the ground, since you won't be at a station platform. Get away from the tracks in case another train is coming.

WHAT TO DO IF YOUR VEHICLE GETS STUCK ON THE TRACKS

Get out immediately and call 911 and the railroad's 800 number posted at the crossing to alert authorities. If you see a train coming, run toward it and off to the side to avoid being hit by debris from the collision.

SAFETY FIRST
Motor vehicle crashes
—most of which are
preventable—are the
leading cause of death
among U.S. teens.

HOW TO SURVIVE A

CAR CRASH

ACT FAST WHEN THERE'S AN ENGINE FIRE, YOUR BRAKES FAIL OR AFTER YOU GO AIRBORNE

> You may think you are the best driver in the world, but it still won't necessarily prevent an accident. Keep your eyes on distracted drivers and improve your own road skills to keep your Firebird from becoming a fireball.

SCARY STATISTICS
Traffic accidents
kill as many as 40,000
Americans and cost the U.S.
nearly $900 billion a year.

WEAR YOUR BELT PROPERLY

Half of all accident fatalities could be
prevented if seat belts are worn correctly,
according to the National Highway Traffic
Safety Administration. The shoulder harness
should be tight and the lap belt should sit low
across the hips, not the stomach. And make
sure all your passengers do the same.

PREVENT PROJECTILES

Stow that bag of groceries in the trunk;
ditto for anything else you'd rather not
have hit you in the head. Invest in a car
harness for your dog.

SERVICE THE CAR REGULARLY

Bring your car to the shop for regular
checkups. If your brake or airbag light
comes on, get to your mechanic; you'll want
them to be working if the worst happens.

ADJUST YOUR POSITION

Sit up straight; adjust the headrest so it sits close
to the back of your head. Adjust the steering
wheel and move the seat so you can reach
the pedals without straining. This position is
the one at which the car's safety equipment is
designed to protect you.

HAVE ESCAPE TOOLS HANDY

A pocket knife, a seat belt cutter, a glass
breaker, a small flashlight…any of these
may help you get out of your car if someone
smashes into you. Pick them up at your auto-
supply store and stash them in your glove box.
A small first-aid kit is also essential.

KEEP YOUR PHONE CHARGED

Get an extra charger pack and keep that
charged, too. Call 911 if you're in an accident,
or if you see another accident take place.

YOUR CAR FLIPS

As you feel the car turning, take your feet off the pedals, release the steering wheel, cross your arms, hold your shoulders and push yourself into the seat. Once you come to halt, pause and get your bearings. Check yourself for head injuries, cuts or broken bones. If you're injured, stay where you are until help arrives. Don't remove the seat belt too quickly; that little head-down fall could kill you. Reach down and brace yourself against the car ceiling while pushing your feet on the floor. Carefully unlatch the buckle and crawl toward the door. If it opens, get out and move far away from the vehicle in case it catches on fire. If you can't get through the door, then look for your phone to call for help. Otherwise, wait for the police. The first few minutes after a rollover are the most dangerous. You'll be disoriented and may not realize you're walking into traffic.

YOUR BRAKES FAIL

Honk and turn on the hazard lights to alert other drivers. Check for an obstruction by pumping the pedal—you may have a bottle or can under it you can kick away. Take your foot off the gas. On an automatic, slowly lower one gear at a time. With a stick, downshift two gears at a time. Don't put the car in neutral as you'll lose engine braking, and don't turn off the car as you'll lose power steering. On cars with anti-lock brakes, press the pedal to the floor to engage the electronically controlled brakes. If you have regular brakes, pump the pedal a few times to build up brake fluid pressure, then slowly apply the parking brake. This could put the car into a skid; if so, turn into it, working your way to the right lane, or onto dirt or a gravel shoulder.

THE ENGINE IGNITES

At the first hint of smoke or burning plastic, pull over and turn off the engine to prevent a small fire from becoming a big one. If smoke is already filling the car, crack a window, as the fumes can cause you to lose consciousness. Then get out fast. Don't try to douse the fire yourself or open the hood: The metal will burn your fingers and the air will fan the flames.

FATAL INFERNOS
Nearly 20 percent of all fires in the U.S. involve vehicles.

NIGHTMARE CRUISE
The captain of the doomed *Concordia* got a prison term for manslaughter and abandoning ship.

HOW TO SURVIVE A

SHIPWRECK

WHEN YOU GET THAT SINKING FEELING, KNOW HOW TO KEEP YOUR HEAD ABOVE WATER

> Almost exactly 100 years after the *HMS Titanic* hit an iceberg and sank, killing nearly 1,500 people, the Italian cruise ship *Costa Concordia* hit underwater rocks, leaving 32 people dead in 2012. The grim lesson: Ocean liners still go down. But that doesn't mean you have to go down with them.

FAST FACT

The *Titanic*'s lifeboats had seats for one-third of the 2,224 on board, which at the time exceeded British safety codes.

THINK FIRST, ACT NEXT

Don't race for the lifeboat or jump into the water. Stay on the boat or ship as long as possible—help may arrive long before the vessel sinks. But if it doesn't, your first priority is getting a life vest or other flotation device. You will not be able to tread water for very long.

ABANDON SHIP

When you prepare to jump off the ship, jump from the high side, so the boat doesn't crush you when it finally capsizes. Because your body will hit the water hard, jump from as low a height as possible. The ideal distance is less than 15 feet.

JUMP PROPERLY

Don't dive headfirst into the water. Keep your shoes on, hold your nose with one hand while grasping your abdomen with the other, then jump with your legs crossed. Make sure you have a clear path and that there are no people or boats in the water.

SWIM AWAY QUICKLY

Once you hit the water, swim away from the boat as fast as you can. You want to avoid any debris that's falling from the ship and the suction effect caused by its sinking. What's more, oil tanks can rupture once the ship goes under, so it's imperative to get as far away as fast as possible so as not to be consumed by the flames.

AVOID HYPOTHERMIA

Due to water's higher density, it'll cool your body 20 times faster than air, making hypothermia the biggest threat (after drowning). Hug your knees to your body or wrap your arms around other people to preserve body heat.

DON'T DRINK SEAWATER

The salt will cause dehydration. Try to capture rainwater or dew in tarps. Even if you have provisions, go easy on the food—it will only make you thirsty. You can live a lot longer without food than without water.

I Survived...
A CAPSIZED BOAT

On February 4, 1992, Ron Walker Jr. was returning on the 90-foot fishing boat *The Stardust* with a load of mackerel and herring to transfer the catch to a Russian ship at the mouth of the Delaware Bay. Then the winds picked up, the waves grew strong and suddenly the boat started to sink.

After I knew I couldn't save the boat, I was worried about getting out of there. The water pressure kept knocking me down the stairs, and the boat started going over on its side. I pulled myself up to the wheelhouse, where the rest of my gang was.

As soon as the boat started rolling, we started climbing and crawling on the side of the boat until it was completely capsized. We were sitting on the keel when the Russians started throwing us lines. If we hadn't crawled to the side of the boat like that while it was rolling, we would have been in the water—and the water was 30 degrees.

I didn't go back on a boat like that for a while.

I bought a little day boat and went conching for a year and a half. But then I went back. I had to do something, and I knew the business better than anything else. Plus, when you get a big set—I'm talking, like, 100 ton of fish and you see them jumping in the net—it's exciting. The money's not bad, either.

The whole experience changed me a lot. I realized how quickly stuff happens. I mean, that boat sank in 15 minutes. I realized I was lucky to be alive.

CHAPTER 06

DOOMSDAY

> The COVID-19 epidemic made many of us believe a postapocalyptic world seemed less science fiction and more tomorrow's headlines. Fight fear by learning how to survive a global pandemic, weapons of mass destruction and a nuclear meltdown.

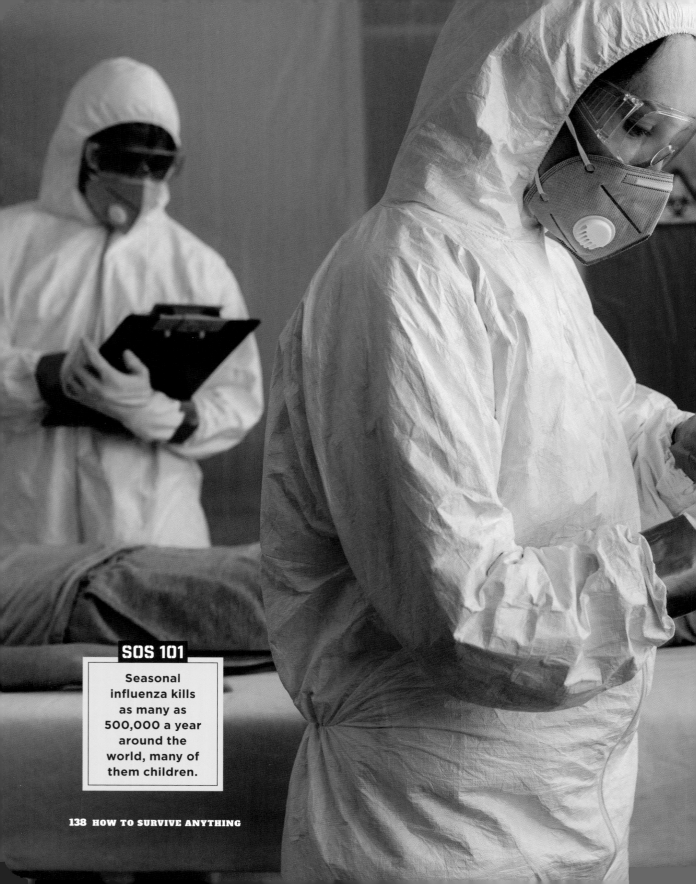

HOW TO SURVIVE A
GLOBAL PANDEMIC

WHEN DISEASE BECOMES A WEAPON OF MASS DESTRUCTION, IT'S IMPORTANT TO BE SELF-SUFFICIENT

BACK TO BASICS Health experts say simple measures—like regularly washing your hands—can dramatically curb disease outbreaks.

In December 2019, the first known case of COVID-19, also known as the novel coronavirus, was documented in Wuhan, China, according to a January 2020 study in the journal *The Lancet*. About three months later, the World Health Organization labeled the coronavirus a global pandemic. Entire cities were shut down, professional sports and concerts canceled, and travel across borders banned completely, in the hopes of putting the brakes on the potentially deadly disease. It echoed outbreaks of the past, but on a much larger and more modern scale—and experts say the biggest lesson we can learn is to plan for the worst.

139

LIMIT YOUR EXPOSURE

According to Stephanie Sterling, MD, section chief of infectious diseases and hospital epidemiologist at NYU Langone Hospital-Brooklyn in NYC, some types of viruses can be transmitted by touching an infected surface—especially highly contagious ones like coronavirus. Because of that history, it's important to take extra precautions like these to stay healthy.

Wash your hands. If there's only one tactic you use, this is the one to choose, says Sterling. "Practice very frequent hand hygiene; make it a priority," she advises.

"That means before eating, after being on public transportation or in other public spaces, and especially after being around people who've been sneezing or coughing." The Centers for Disease Control and Prevention (CDC) adds that you should also wash your hands after using the toilet, before and after treating a cut or wound, after touching an animal and after touching garbage.

To practice the most effective hand-washing, wet your hands with clean, running hot water, turn off the tap and then apply soap. Lather your hands, including between your fingers and under your nails, for at least 20 seconds. (That's about the time

HOW TO USE PROTECTIVE GEAR

Protective gear is only as good as the way you use it. And there is most definitely a right and a wrong way to put on (don) and remove (doff) your personal protective equipment (PPE). Follow these steps to make sure you and your family stay safe:

DONNING PPE

All protective gear should be put on before entering a patient's room.
Gown Pull on the gown and tie it securely.
Mask Secure the mask on your face and check the fit.
Eyes Put on goggles or face mask.
Gloves Pull on, extending their wrists so that they cover the cuffs of the gown.

DOFFING PPE

Always assume the outer surfaces of your PPE have been contaminated and behave accordingly. Everything other than the mask should be removed before leaving the room and placed into a covered container. Keep the mask on until you're out the door, then remove and discard in a covered container near the door.
Gloves Grab one glove near the wrist and peel it off, turning it inside out, then hold it in your gloved hand. Remove the second glove by sliding your fingers under the wrist, turning it inside out as it peels off.
Eyes Remove eye protection by holding it by the strap or earpieces.
Gowns Untie the gown and pull it away from your body by touching only the inner surface at the neck, then ball it up for disposal.
Mask Remove by grasping by the straps and pulling it off.

ALTERNATIVE

Leave gloves on and untie gown, then grab front of gown with gloved hands and pull it off. As it comes away, pull hands from the gloves, turning them, and gown, inside out. Then remove eye protection and mask as above.

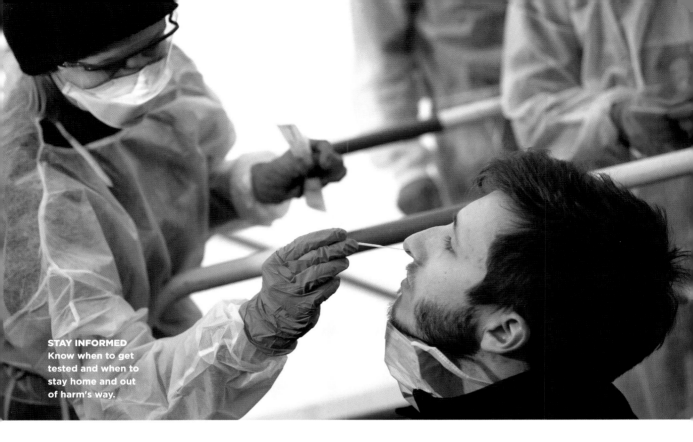

it takes to sing "Happy Birthday" twice.) Scrub vigorously, as if you were about to perform surgery, getting down into the webbing between your fingers and scrubbing your thumbs and palms. Then rinse under clean, running water and use a paper towel to dry your hands, then turn off the tap while holding the towel.

Use hand sanitizer. The CDC notes that the soap-and-water method of handwashing is the best way to get rid of germs, but if that's not available, it's also OK to use a hand-sanitizer product that's at least 60 percent alcohol. During the coronavirus outbreak, hand sanitizers were one of the first things to disappear off store shelves, making it difficult for many people to access. (See "DIY Hand Sanitizer" on page 145 for details on how to make your own.)

Avoid touching your face. According to Andres Romero, MD, an infectious-disease specialist at Providence Saint John's Health Center in Santa Monica, California, this is another top strategy for preventing viruses from getting into your system. Many people increase their exposure by having germs on their hands and then rubbing their eyes, nose or mouth, which allows the germs— including viruses—to enter the body. Can't break the habit? Try keeping your hands busy with a stress ball, fiddling with a rubber band around your wrist or even tucking your hands under your legs while sitting.

Clean surfaces thoroughly. Scientists may not yet know whether the virus causing the pandemic can live on surfaces, but it pays to be extra diligent about hygiene. Choose cleaning products that disinfect as well as

BIOLOGICAL WARFARE

A 1993 study by the U.S. Office of Technology Assessment called biological agents "true weapons of mass destruction with a potential for lethal mayhem that can exceed that of nuclear weapons." Despite the terrifying prospect of germ warfare, other studies insist the threat of global annihilation is minimal. Although biological agents are theoretically cheap and easy to deploy, they are notoriously fragile, with limited life spans, and can be destroyed or weakened by heat and oxygen. As such, they are difficult to package and stockpile. If they are delivered in some sort of bomb, the blast will likely kill the organisms. If they were to be dumped into the drinking water supply, it would have to be in amounts too large to acquire and store. This explains why these things only happen in movies. Still, a smaller attack is possible. As a 1999 CDC report says, "The threat of bioterrorism, in which biological agents are used by extremists as weapons against civilian populations, generates considerable anxiety."

clean, or use diluted bleach or hydrogen peroxide. Remember never to mix bleach with ammonia—the combination can generate toxic vapors. One more common virus that does live on surfaces is influenza, so you'll be protecting yourself against that bug in the process.

Limit contact with people who are sick. You can lower your exposure to many viral illnesses by limiting contact, if possible, with those who are ill. If you are around people who are sick, be even more diligent about washing your hands and not touching your face. Think of alternatives to areas that might have numerous sick people. For example, consider using a nurse hotline or online consultation instead of going to a clinic, or choose the drive-thru window of a pharmacy rather than sitting in the waiting area for your prescription. If you do have to go to a clinic, arrive close to the time of your appointment to limit how long you'll be waiting there—and of course, be sure to wash your hands thoroughly after leaving.

SUPPORT YOUR IMMUNE SYSTEM
Whenever there's a threat of severe illness, it's important to keep your immune system strong to help fend off viral attacks. That's particularly important if you have ongoing health issues that tend to make you more vulnerable to catching other illnesses—for example, if you have diabetes, asthma, heart disease, metabolic disorders or cancer. And even if you don't have an existing health concern, strategies like these can be helpful for making your immune system more resilient and effective.

Make small changes. When it comes to supporting your immune system, one healthy habit like eating better, moving more or getting a bit of extra shut-eye can have a ripple effect, according to Frank Hu, MD, PhD, professor and chair of the Department of Nutrition at Harvard T.H. Chan School of Public Health. For example, research has shown that having a regular sleep schedule of seven to nine hours per night can prompt healthier eating habits and give you more energy to exercise consistently. These habits can also lower stress, which is crucial for staying healthy, since stress responses in the

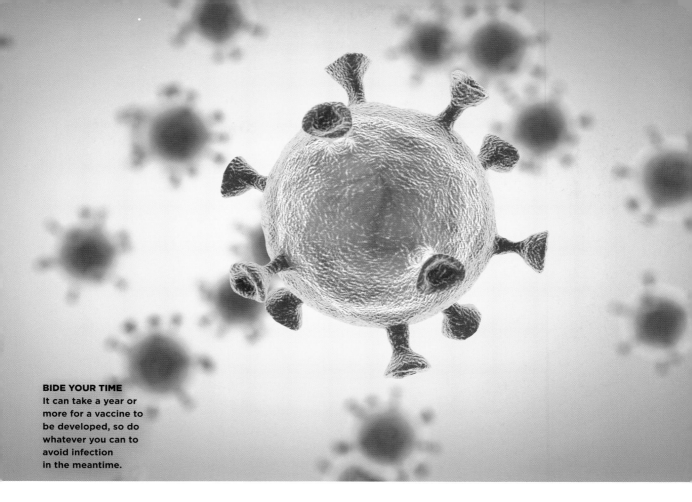

BIDE YOUR TIME
It can take a year or more for a vaccine to be developed, so do whatever you can to avoid infection in the meantime.

body can decrease immune function. "In addition to protecting your immediate health, habits like these help with long-term quality of life and well-being, too," says Hu.

Spend time outside. There are several studies that connect being outdoors in fresh air with a stronger immune system. In part, that's due to lower stress levels, but researchers have also noted that sunlight increases levels of vitamin D—boosting mood and a feeling of well-being—and that chemicals released by plants, called phytoncides, have a significantly beneficial effect on immune system function.

Practice good kitchen habits. Wash all fruits and vegetables, and cook meat thoroughly before consuming. There's no evidence that

COVID-19 is spread through undercooked meats or unwashed produce, but Romero notes that these strategies are good practices in general for avoiding food poisoning, which can put your immune system at risk.

Get a flu shot. It may not work against mutated strains or viruses, but it can't hurt. Also stock up on antiviral medications, prescription and nonprescription drugs and other health supplies, including a first aid kit and pain relievers. Limit the amount of antibiotics you take to decrease resistance.

STOCK UP ON SUPPLIES
Before a pandemic spreads, prepare your home by stocking up on food, water and medical supplies. Do this sooner rather than

later, as store shelves will likely go bare once panic sets in.

Keep plenty of bottled water around.

Keep in mind that while water doesn't go bad, plastic eventually breaks down and leaches into chemicals, so try to store water in glass containers if at all possible. Have enough to last you at least four weeks, and longer if possible, or make sure you have a source of fresh water that is filtered or otherwise safe to drink.

Shore up your pantry. Like water, you should have enough nonperishable food to last you at least four weeks, longer if possible. Shelf-stable foods that don't require cooking are best in an emergency. (For more, see page 168). Try to include the following items:

- Ready-to-eat canned meats, fruits and vegetables
- Protein and fruit bars
- Dry cereal or granola
- Peanut or other nut butters
- Dried fruit
- Canned juices
- Non-perishable pasteurized milk
- High energy foods
- Food for infants
- Comfort/stress foods

Add on some protective gear. Buy a big box of disposable medical masks. During the coronavirus outbreak, stocks quickly ran short. The face mask most commonly recommended is the N95 respirator, which has been tested to block at least 95 percent of all test particles

EMERGENCY EQUIPMENT

Should you be unable to locate the protective gear you want, there are a few ways you can make do with what you have available. Keep in mind: These options are all vastly inferior to using the proper equipment, so save these suggestions for when the real deal isn't accessible.

MASK

Cover your mouth and nose with cloth, perhaps layered with a coffee filter or something similar. Anything you can do to limit the amount of contaminants that can reach your mucous membranes, the better. Again, this is far from ideal, but it is better than nothing.

EYE PROTECTION

Hardware stores carry several types of clear plastic helmet-type masks that cover the face. These are often used when operating grinders and similar types of power equipment.

GOWNS

Tyvek suits might be a more inexpensive alternative. They are sold for use when cleaning up hazardous waste or dealing with harsh chemicals. Select one that has elastic cuffs, as they will provide better protection. However, be aware that these suits aren't heavy-duty at all and can puncture or tear easily. Great care must be used when the suit is worn.

GLOVES

In a pinch, rubber gloves like those used for washing dishes are better than bare hands when dealing with infected people or contaminated items. Be sure they don't have any rips or tears.

down to 0.3 micron in size. Add goggles with vents and coating to prevent fogging up and nitrile gloves that can help protect people who are sensitive to latex.

Disinfect and wipe down. Boost your supplies of cleaning equipment. Use disinfecting wipes or sprays to kill viruses and bacteria that live on surfaces, or try a solution made with 1½ cups of bleach to 1 gallon of water. Wipe down the surfaces in your home (including the remote control and your phone). To kill germs in clothing, sheets and towels, wash in hot water with a color-safe bleach detergent.

Keep germs away. Get some plastic sheeting with duct tape to seal windows and Tyvek coveralls with foot and head coverings.

DESIGNATE A SAFE ROOM
Since you'll want to avoid close contact with people who are sick—and you won't know who is infected—you will need to stay away from everyone outside of your home, and there may be members of your own family who are affected.

Make a sick room. To be prepared, you must have the ability to voluntarily self-quarantine. To avoid the spread of disease, set up a "sick room" in your home to separate infected people from the rest of the house. Make sure to seal off air-conditioning and heating ducts to prevent the spread of bacteria and viruses to other rooms in the house. Be sure to include forms of entertainment like magazines and books as well as medical supplies.

Keep contact to a minimum. Only one person should be allowed to enter the sick room to bring food and water and offer care. That person should wear protective coveralls, gloves, goggles and a mask and disinfect

DIY HAND SANITIZER

One of the most unexpected developments of the coronavirus outbreak in the U.S. was the sudden depletion of hand sanitizer. Within just a few days, it was almost impossible to purchase a bottle for personnel use. But it is easy to DIY your own, with recipes like the one below. Keep in mind that for the hand sanitizer to be effective, it needs to contain at least 60 percent alcohol.

INGREDIENTS
⅔ cup rubbing alcohol
⅓ cup aloe vera gel

Combine ingredients in bowl and stir. Decant into clean bottle or soap dispenser. Be sure to cover your hands thoroughly with the sanitizer and let them air dry.

everything afterward. Stock the room with disposable plates, cups and tableware, and disinfect the room each day.

Clean up quickly. Keep a covered trash container just inside the door and immediately place disposable items into it prior to leaving the room. (See "How to Use Protective Gear" on page 140 for the right order in which to remove PPE.) Hands and faces should be washed in the nearest bathroom. Waste should be removed and disposed of daily.

COLLISION COURSE
When atoms are split,
they release huge
amounts of energy.

HOW TO SURVIVE A

NUCLEAR BLAST

TIME TO THINK ABOUT THE UNTHINKABLE

> North Korea has a sophisticated nuclear weapons and ballistic missile program, and is not afraid to show the world its strength. In July 2017, it tested its first intercontinental ballistic missile; two months later it conducted a test on what it claimed was a thermonuclear weapon. If the worst were to occur, outside of the immediate blast radius of about a mile, an explosion could be survivable—assuming you're prepared and know what to do in the moment.

STOCK UP ON SUPPLIES

"Weave preparedness into the fabric of your neighborhood and it will ultimately help you be more resilient," says Michelle Constant, the founder of emergency management firm Constant & Associates, who recommends people stash seven days of food and water, plus flashlights, a battery-operated radio and extra doses of prescription medications. Some families will have other specific needs, such as pet supplies or specialized medical equipment.

Make a disaster plan for your neighborhood: Identify people who might need immediate additional help; who have CPR or medical training; who own equipment that can move debris.

HEED OFFICIAL WARNINGS AND INSTRUCTIONS

The moment a nuclear blast takes place will be one of terror and confusion. People will find out in a variety of ways, including opt-in text messages and emails from local government, and if available, an alert siren. The Emergency Alert System might be activated, interrupting all radio and TV programming to provide any known information about the attack, detailed instructions on what to do next, and messages from the White House.

With the actual blast, some people might see a spherical fireball; others might feel the blast waves first and mistake it for an earthquake, depending on how close they are to the blast.

FAST FACT

It would take five minutes from the time the president orders a missile strike for the weapons to be launched from silos or submarines.

YOU SHOULD GET A WARNING

It would take about 90 minutes for a North Korean intercontinental ballistic missile (ICBM) to reach the United States. Launched in a high, arcing trajectory, the missile would spend most of that time above the atmosphere. This is where the U.S. would try to destroy the missile with the $40 billion Ground-Based Midcourse Defense (GMD) system. Practice sessions have not been overly encouraging, failing to blow up fake warheads in six of 10 tests since 2004, although the more recent tests have been a success.

FIRST SECONDS BEFORE A BOMB IMPACT

Monitor official reports as you seek cover in the strongest structure possible, preferably deep in a building behind heavy concrete walls. Even huddling behind a concrete wall can protect you from the initial shock waves. Your fate depends on where you are. With a likely blast radius of about a mile, the nuclear weapon will cause massive damage and potentially kill millions of people.

If you're in this zone you will probably not survive. Even another mile or two away in the "light damage" zone, the blast will inflict significant damage.

WHAT TO DO IN THE FIRST 15 MINUTES

If you're still outside during impact, seek shelter immediately. You have about 10 to 15 minutes before radioactive debris rains down. High doses of radiation cause vomiting, blisters skin, burns lungs, damages bone marrow and leads to diseases like leukemia. If you're exposed, take off contaminated clothing and brush the particles from your hair. Shower with soap if possible.

SOS 101

The old-fashioned "duck and cover" drills from elementary school are actually considered an effective protection against flying glass and debris from a nuclear blast wave.

AFTER AN HOUR, THE WAITING GAME BEGINS

Radiation levels decrease quickly— nearly half of its power is gone in the first hour—so remain indoors. Continue to monitor updates on an emergency radio for the location of radioactive clouds that could be blowing your way, or to learn if there's another missile strike coming.

149

TICKING TIME BOMB
Yellowstone's 300 geysers make up two-thirds of all the geysers on Earth.

NATURE COULD CAUSE A NUCLEAR WINTER

While we worry about a North Korean missile, Mother Nature may have her own plans. Deep beneath a caldera in Yellowstone National Park lurks a vast reservoir of magma that will one day blast out in a supervolcano. One thousand times as powerful as the 1980 Mount St. Helens eruption, it would plunge the United States into a nuclear winter.

SHOULD WE WORRY?
It has lain dormant for more than 70,000 years, a blink of a geological eye, but signs now point to another blast occurring within centuries based on that reservoir refilling faster than previously thought. "It's shocking how little time is required to take a volcanic system from being quiet and sitting there to the edge of an eruption," Hannah Shamloo, a co-author of a study on the volcano, told *The New York Times*. When Yellowstone blows its top and submerges surrounding areas in molten rock, it would kill as many as 90,000 people instantly and lead to economic disaster with effects felt around the world.

KEEPING TRACK
Although scientists'
high-tech monitors can
pick up on the slightest
of the caldera's mood
changes, they would
not have a lot of time
to react. National Park
geologist Hank Hessler
has said their monitors
can only accurately
predict if an eruption
is imminent within a
two-week span.

The iconic mushroom cloud likely won't
be visible until several minutes after the
explosion, when it's too late to take cover.

WHAT TO DO RIGHT AWAY
Disaster experts use the phrase "time,
distance, shielding" to refer to the three
most important aspects of making it
through a nuclear event. All will come
into play the moment you learn of a blast.

"For a time, make sure you limit
your exposure to the threat," Constant
says, as radiation tends to lose its intensity
quickly. Get as low in a structure as possible,
crouching behind something thick like a
concrete wall, and, if possible, trying to
protect yourself behind lead. Any kind of
protection is better than none.

It's critical to stay where you are and not
go outside for at least 24 hours because,
as ready.gov points out, "radiation levels
are extremely dangerous after a nuclear
detonation but the levels reduce rapidly."

If you are outside when a blast hits, don't
look at the flash, stay down and get behind
any cover you can. Afterward, remove any
clothing you were wearing, which will be
radioactive, put it in a sealed bag and get
clean with soap and water as soon as possible.

**HOW TO DEAL WITH THE
DEVASTATING AFTERMATH**
It would likely be a few days before FEMA
could bring aid. There would also be a
significant economic effect for the country
—one study claimed the economic cost
of one atomic bomb detonating over
New York City would be $10 trillion.

The country would be gripped by a state
of panic, likely for some time. But Constant
believes such a state can be "mitigated with
information and access to resources." Experts
agree that a better-prepared community will
be better off to survive and rebuild.

MILES OF TERROR
A damaged reactor at Three Mile Island in Middletown, Pennsylvania, in 1999 stoked fears of a massive radiation leak.

HOW TO SURVIVE A

NUCLEAR MELTDOWN

THREE MILE ISLAND AND CHERNOBYL OFFER LESSONS IN RESPONDING TO A NUCLEAR EMERGENCY

In the Ukraine city of Pripyat, all the clocks are stopped at 11:55 a.m. That's when the electricity was cut off after the nearby Chernobyl nuclear plant explosion on April 26, 1986. Now a ghost town, Pripyat shows that a nuclear accident can be survived —but at great cost.

GET AWAY FROM THE TROUBLE

Follow official instructions for evacuation. The radiation is strongest immediately after a disaster, so you may be told to put distance between you and the plant as soon as possible. If driving away, keep the windows rolled up and the air on recycle. If you're advised to stay indoors, turn off vents and air conditioners. Go to the most protected part of the house, like a basement.

WHEN TO SEEK MEDICAL HELP

If you're exposed to radiation, stash your clothes in a bag, seal it and take a shower. If you suffer radiation-exposure symptoms like nausea or blistering, get to the hospital. Evacuees should heed official instructions on when it's safe to go home. Radiation loses its intensity quickly.

MAKE DIFFICULT DECISIONS

After Chernobyl, officials debated how long to wait before people could return to hard-hit areas. Wildlife, however, has flourished in Pripyat since then. You can measure the amount of radiation in the air with a Geiger counter—not a bad purchase if you live near a power plant.

VAST DESTRUCTION
The Chernobyl Nuclear power plant suffered massive damage in a 1986 explosion

SOS 101

People near a nuclear plant may not be asked to evacuate during an accident. The wind direction plays a factor.

IN THE AFTERMATH
Responders with radiation-
protective clothing
searched for bodies after
an earthquake and tsunami
struck the Fukushima
Daiichi Nuclear Power
Plant in 2011.

155

CHAPTER 07

SURVIVAL 101

❯ That first responder might not get to you right away. Long before rescuers roll up, survival will depend on you. Pack a "go-bag" of essential disaster items, draft a family emergency plan, stock a first-aid kit and learn basic lifesaving skills. Natural disasters and other threats are the new normal. Don't be left behind.

ON THE ROAD
If you decide to leave, do so as early as you safely can to avoid the heaviest traffic.

EXPRESS LANES
END
1/2 MILE

SOS 101

A fully equipped and robust bug-out vehicle could turn out to be a very wise investment.

DO YOU STAY OR GO?

HOW TO KNOW WHEN TO BUG OUT

> When the unthinkable happens, you have to decide whether to stay where you are or head to what you hope is a better and safer location. The key word here is "hope"—because the place you are heading to may be no better than the place you are leaving. In fact, it could actually be worse. Deciding to move is a big step and one you should not take lightly. The trick, if there is one, is to plan, plan and plan some more. Your very life could depend on it.

THE PLAN

Deciding to do something at the last minute is never a good thing. While we all hope that nothing bad happens, we have to be prepared just in case it does. Part of that preparedness is having a plan. What will you do? Where will you go? Can you get there safely? How will you get there? Who will you bring with you? All of these questions have to be answered well before you have to put a plan into action. In most cases one plan will not be enough. Make sure you have a plan B and even a plan C in place. You can't put all of your eggs in one basket. You have to have multiple locations mapped out in case you need to bug out. Your first choice may not

work out for any number of reasons.

Part of your plan should include who you intend to work with. Face the fact that you can't do it alone, not for long anyway. In a doomsday situation, you will need to defend what you have, hunt, fish, forage and do whatever it takes to stay alive. What happens if you get sick or hurt? There is safety in numbers—and some extra help will mean you have a better chance of surviving.

Is your group going to be just your family, or are you going to include friends and neighbors? Keep in mind that every person you include in your group must be able to bring something to the table. If they can't, they become a potential liability. What they bring could be extra food and water or even

PREPARATION MUST-HAVES

These survival essentials should be in your vehicle at all times, just in case you need to hit the road quickly.

HIGH-QUALITY KNIVES

No tool is more valuable than a good, high-quality, stout knife. Multifunction ones are good to have around in a pinch, but you might also want a serrated blade for cutting.

WATER FILTRATION

Most water is questionable, so you'll need to filter it. There are many different portable water-filtration available that will fit your needs.

FIRE-STARTING

Without fire you have no way to cook food, boil water or keep warm. Carry multiple ways of starting fires with you; these should include portable lighters, matches, flint and steel for different options under various conditions.

MEDICAL

Medical emergencies will arise—everything from open wounds to sprains and insect bites. Every person should carry a personal first-aid kit, and a full medical-supply pack should be located at your base camp or in your car.

COMMUNICATION

Some way to communicate with the outside world and your team is vital. Two-way and satellite radios can work when other options won't.

PERSONAL DEFENSE

There are bad people out there, so some sort of personal-defense weapon should be within reach at all times.

CORDAGE

Cordage is essential for a host of purposes, including shelter-building, setting snares, fixing snowshoes and binding wounds.

STAY IN TOUCH
Make sure a team
member always
has a way of
communicating
with home base.

161

extra fuel to keep the generators working. Perhaps it is expertise in areas that you happen to be weak in. All of this should be considered.

Everyone in your party needs to be kept abreast of the plan and any changing conditions. Discuss every step with every member of the group. They all need to know their specific role, where supplies are kept, where to meet and when. This is a team effort—and each team member needs to do their part if you are all going to succeed.

STAY WHEN POSSIBLE

Your first plan should always be to stay in place. Unless compromised, the home is always the best bet—if you have prepared. Your home is where most of your supplies of food and water are located. You know your home like the back of your hand, so it is easily defendable from intruders looking to take what you have. You probably have generators and extra fuel to keep them running. You have multiple ways to cook food and boil water, even if you have no power. In other words, you have everything you need to survive in one central location. Most importantly, you have a shelter that will keep you and your supplies safe.

If you stay, and your home is going to be your safe place, it is very important to bring your group to that one central location. It is far easier to keep things under control this way. Take stock of what you have and what you don't. Devise a pecking order. Who is going to be the leader? Who is going to be in charge of food, medical and other areas? The group leader will need to be prepared to make the hard decisions if and when the time comes. It could be deciding to ration food and water, or it could be making the decision to move.

BUG OUT WHEN NECESSARY

Deciding to move can be a scary one. If you have planned ahead correctly, then you have a few places to head to. This needs to be part of your plan. Plot out the escape routes you will take if you have to move. Having more than one way out is a must. If you do decide to go, you have to realize that you can't take everything you have with you. Be prepared to move quickly when you have made the decision to leave.

If you have to go, you want to get as far away from the danger as you can, and in as safe a manner as you can. Hopefully, you can get out using a vehicle of some sort, but this may not be an option. Are you prepared to carry what you need on your back if you have to? Every member of your family or party needs to help carry the load, with food and water being the top priorities.

Wherever you're heading, you should make sure it is safer than the place you're leaving. Does it have the things you will require, or do you need to bring everything with you? If you planned ahead, then the area you are going to should have caches of supplies already there. Even so, you should bring whatever you can.

If you can get there by vehicle, make sure your fuel tank is full, and bring as much extra fuel with you as you can. Gas may be hard to come by, if available it's even at all. Load your vehicle with food, water, weapons, ammo and medical supplies, because you never know what you will find when you get there. Someone may have already been there and may have found and depleted your caches. Hope for the best, but be prepared for the worst. Leave behind all items that are not essential to survival. Team up with other members in your party and spread out the load.

If you have to walk out, the amount of supplies you can take with you is limited to

MAP IT OUT
Bugging out means you'd better know where you're going and how you're getting there.

what you and the other members in your party can carry. Leave the canned food and heavy goods behind and stick to much lighter freeze-dried food. Bring as much water as you can carry; there will never be enough water. Medical supplies should be part of the equation.

WHAT REALLY MATTERS

The decision to stay or to go is a difficult one. Both choices have their pros and cons. With proper planning, you will be able to decide which is best for you and the situation you are presented with. Those who plan will have a much better chance at survival.

163

STAY IN PLACE
A bomb shelter in the backyard might be a great idea in some cases, but you don't need to hide in a hole in the ground to be safe.

HUNKERING DOWN

WHAT YOU'LL NEED WHILE SHELTERING AT HOME

> In most crisis situations (and most definitely when dealing with a global public-health emergency), sheltering in place at home is going to be your best option. That's where we feel comfortable and safe. We know the area and the people around us. Our home is where we've stockpiled our gear and supplies, so it just makes sense to stay with our investment, rather than attempt to transport it elsewhere. Plus, by hunkering down, we lessen the possibility of exposing ourselves to other dangers on the roads. There are, of course, some emergency scenarios where evacuation is the better option, such as when a wildfire is encroaching on your neighborhood or a hurricane is eyeballing your town for landfall. Here's what you need to make sure you're prepared when you stay in place.

DISINFECTANT

Killing germs at home can be an important line of defense against illness, especially when you're sheltering in place or trying to avoid public contact while a deadly disease is spreading. How you clean your house, and with which ingredients, is also key. More thorough than paper towels and sponges, disinfecting wipes like those made by Clorox and Lysol are convenient, and the companies claim the wipes kill 99.9 percent of viruses and bacteria.

If you're facing a pandemic, bigger guns may be required. The best, most thorough germ-killer is bleach. Using a solution of 1½ cups of bleach to 1 gallon of water, wipe down the surfaces in your home, including frequently touched items like switch plates, phones and TV remotes. Let the bleach solution sit on the surface for at least 10 minutes. To kill germs in clothing, sheets and towels, wash them in hot water with a color-safe bleach detergent.

WATER

Every preparedness plan begins with water. Having a source for clean water makes everything else so much easier. The problem is that water is heavy and bulky. It can't be made any lighter and it can't be made any smaller. One gallon of water weighs 8.34 pounds. It's not a lot in the grand scheme of things, but the weight adds up quickly when you start storing water. A case of 24 half-liter bottles comes to a little more than 3 gallons of water, enough for one person for a couple of days. But if you're looking at prepping for a month or more, that's a lot of bottles to have sitting in the basement.

Consider a multipronged approach to water. Have some water stored but also have the means to filter or purify water you can source from outside. Sawyer, MSR and Seychelle are three trusted brand names in the filtration business.

COMMUNICATION

People can only make informed decisions if they seek out information about the situation. Take the time to get a ham radio license and acquire the gear necessary to communicate with the world around you. Even if you just listen in without broadcasting, you'll be able to make better decisions. Another option is to pick up a good radio that will tune in AM/FM as well as shortwave transmissions. Consider investing in a radio that can be powered by crank or solar power in addition to standard batteries.

STORAGE

You can have all the supplies in the world, but if they aren't stored properly they'll be of no use to you. The same general rules apply no matter what the item is. Keep it cool, dry and away from sunlight. Heat and moisture are usually what limits storage life. A dry basement is often the first choice. Another option might be a spare bedroom.

Many people have very limited storage space, so creativity becomes necessary. Under the beds is a possibility, as is the back of a closet. Or try installing a shelf on the inside of the closet, right above the door. Boxes or totes of supplies can be covered with a tastefully printed fabric and turned into an occasional table in the living room.

Avoid attics; they often get very warm. Same with garages or other outbuildings. Make sure your supplies are kept cool and dry—and reasonably accessible, so you can rotate them as needed.

HYGIENE

Don't forget to stock up on toiletries like deodorant, soap, shampoo, toothpaste, toothbrushes and dental floss. These might not seem truly survival-related, but the cleaner you are, the better protected you are from infections and illnesses.

MEDICAL/FIRST AID

This is an area where you will really want to seek out training in advance. While most of us are very capable of handling bumps, bruises and the occasional small cut, the average person lacks the knowledge to properly handle a compound fracture or a gash that requires stitches. Buying the supplies is the easy part; anyone can do that. Knowing how to use them effectively takes education and training.

A single wound can call for quite a bit of gauze and bandages and a serious injury might require changed bandages several times a day for a few weeks—so keep extra first-aid supplies on hand. Don't forget common over-the-counter remedies for cold symptoms, upset stomach, indigestion and the like. While these don't last forever, they don't instantly become worthless when they hit their expiration dates. They just become less effective as time goes on.

LEARN FIRST AID

That first responder may be you.
Get trained and be prepared

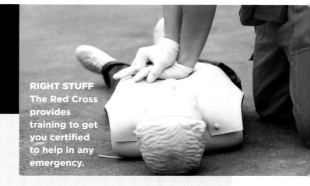

RIGHT STUFF
The Red Cross provides training to get you certified to help in any emergency.

Take a first-aid class to get training for these and other skills that can help you save a life when disaster strikes.

GIVE THE BREATH OF LIFE

When someone suffers a heart attack, their heart stops sending blood to their body. The victim can die in minutes unless a bystander performs CPR (cardiopulmonary resuscitation). To do it, put your hands over a person's heart and push to the beat of "Stayin' Alive" followed by a series of rescue breaths.

Repeat this process until paramedics arrive.

RESCUE A CHOKING VICTIM

If someone is choking (the victim will be unable to talk, but may use the universal sign of choking—hands around the neck) the American Red Cross recommends "a five and five" treatment—deliver five back blows using the heel of your hand between the victim's shoulder blades, followed by five abdominal thrusts (the Heimlich maneuver). Wrap your arms around them with a fist pushed into the soft place between the belly and bottom of the rib cage and thrust upward until whatever's in there is forced out.

TREAT SHOCK

When somebody loses a lot of blood or suffers a major infection or allergic reaction, blood gets cut off to the brain and they become dizzy and pale. Wrap them in a blanket, elevate their feet and put them on their side in case they vomit.

STOCKING YOUR PANTRY

FILL UP YOUR CABINETS AND STAY PREPARED FOR ANY EMERGENCY

When the coronavirus pandemic struck the U.S., many people suddenly found themselves panicking that they would not have enough food on hand (not to mention goods like paper towels and toilet paper!) to weather any shelter-in-place commands. Store shelves were suddenly made bare of items from butter to pasta.

But it doesn't take a pandemic to raise the alarm—even a winter storm can create long lines at the grocery. It's wise to be prepared for any emergency. FEMA (Federal Emergency Management Agency) advises keeping enough supplies on hand to last two weeks, just in case.

WATER

"Having an ample supply of clean water is a top priority in an emergency," notes FEMA. A normally active person needs to consume about a half gallon of water each day—more if you are in a warm climate. Nursing mothers, children and those who are ill may require even more. Aim to store at least one gallon per person per day—or enough for at least two weeks—ideally with bottled water.

SHELF-STABLE FOODS

Some catastrophes lead to power and/or gas outages that render your stove useless, so foods that don't require cooking are best in an emergency. Also, you may not have access to much water, so avoid salty foods that make you thirsty. Consider your family's own needs and tastes—familiar foods can lift morale and offer security in times of stress, notes FEMA. And don't forget nonperishable food for your pets.

Canned foods can be eaten straight out of the container, without being heated, but be sure to have a manual can opener—and never eat from a can that is dented, swollen or corroded. Almost anything labeled with "just add water" is fine. But keep in mind, the fewer steps involved in getting the food ready for consumption, the better. As far as shelf life, in general, things like powdered milk, dried fruit, crackers and potatoes should be used within six months. Canned foods, cereals, peanut butter, jelly and hard candy can last a year or more.

Even with no power you may be able to cook simple dishes. Use grills and camp stoves outdoors only. If you're stuck inside, chafing dishes, fondue pots and fireplaces offer ways to heat up supplies. Dry pasta that only needs to be boiled, coupled with a jar of tomato sauce, makes a fine disaster meal. And stock up on dried beans: They take some time to cook, but cost half as much as canned.

SOS 101

Food poisoning covers a range of foodborne pathogens, with diarrhea and vomiting as the primary symptoms. Consuming contaminated foods, such as spoiled meat or dairy products, is the usual culprit.

DRY CEREAL

CANNED FRUITS & VEGETABLES

VALUE PACK

PURE PROTEIN BAR

CHOCOLATE PEANUT CARAMEL

PROTEIN BARS

RAMEN NOODLES

CANNED TUNA

PERISHABLES

The Red Cross recommends you keep foods like crackers and cookies in sealed containers to make them last longer. Also, it's advisable to empty open packages of sugar, dried fruits and nuts into screw-top jars or airtight containers.

Dry goods will keep longer, but when the power is out, the average refrigerator will only keep food cold for about four hours, provided the door remains closed. That doesn't mean that after that point you need to throw everything out. But it does mean the clock is ticking and perishable food should be eaten soon.

One factor that comes into play is how full the refrigerator and freezer are at the time. The fuller they are, the longer the food will stay cold. When you have power, the refrigerator should be set at about 36°F and the freezer should be at 0°F. Deviating from those temperatures too much shortens the time you have if the power cuts out.

Invest in a thermometer for the refrigerator and another for the freezer. Once the interior of the refrigerator reaches 40°F, you have about two hours before many foods start to get questionable. These include meat and poultry (cooked or uncooked), milk, yogurt, soups, stews and casseroles. Egg dishes can be tricky, too. As a general rule, it is better the food go

into someone's stomach than into the garbage— but if there is any question as to whether the food is still good, toss it. The Department of Homeland Security recommends discarding any food that's been at room temperature for two hours or more.

The freezer is a bit easier. A full freezer will keep your food frozen for about 48 hours. If the freezer is only half full, cut the time in half as well. If you're unsure whether the food is still able to be refrozen safely, check it for ice crystals. If any ice remains, you're good to go.

The takeaway here is realizing that you probably have food in the refrigerator and freezer that you can and should consume before opening the cabinets and cupboards. Just don't take unnecessary risks that might make yourself or your family sick.

LONG-TERM FOODS

Should you wish to explore the world of "survival" food, there are a few options to consider. The first is freeze-dried or dehydrated food usually marketed to hikers. These pouches contain entrees such as beef Stroganoff or chili mac. You add hot water to the pouch and, once the food is rehydrated, dig in. These pouches contain, on average, two servings. The serving sizes vary, but are usually around one cup. Dehydrated foods frequently require boiling

DRIED BEANS

PINTO BEANS
Excellent Source of FIBER

GRANOLA BARS
VALUE PACK
24 BARS
NATURE VALLEY
CRUNCHY

RICE

SPAM
Classic

CANNED MEATS

Chef BOYARDEE
Spaghetti & Meatballs
CANNED PASTA
in Tomato Sauce
NO Preservatives

SKIPPY
CREAMY
PEANUT BUTTER

PEANUT BUTTER

water, as the heat cooks the food while the water rehydrates it. Freeze-dried foods don't require heat, though the taste of something like macaroni and cheese is improved by warming it up.

Another option is to store Meals Ready to Eat, known as MREs. These are based on the rations the United States military issues to the troops. Each MRE comes in a pouch and contains a number of individual components, including an entrée, side dish, crackers or bread, dessert and drink mix. There's also a flameless heater that can be used to warm the food before eating.

Rather than buying the entire MRE, you can buy individual components. Many people purchase just the entrées. MREs are nice because there is nothing that needs to be done to prepare them. They tend to taste better heated, but they don't need to be rehydrated. Still, keep in mind that MREs are expensive when compared to other stored food options. They are also heavier and bulkier.

Start by sampling a few of these options before buying MREs in bulk. Make sure you and your family like the taste and texture, and also ensure the food agrees with you. Better to learn that now rather than in the middle of a disaster.

DEHYDRATED VS. FREEZE-DRIED

The difference between dehydrated and freeze-dried food comes down to the amount of water removed from the food product. Dehydration removes around 90 to 95 percent of moisture from the food. Freeze-drying removes up to 99 percent. Dehydration, whether it's done with a giant machine at a factory or with a home version on your kitchen table, involves circulating heated air around the food, which removes the moisture. For freeze-drying, food is placed in a vacuum chamber and the temperature is lowered to below freezing. The temperature is then slowly raised and, as it comes up, moisture in the food goes from ice to gas.

Overall, they both store very well. The shelf life of most dehydrated food is about 15 to 20 years. Freeze-dried food lasts a little longer, 20 to 25 years. Of course, storage conditions will affect the time frame. As with almost anything you want to store long-term, keep it in a cool, dark and dry place.

ALL ABOARD
Keep your bug-out
bag fully stocked
so you can leave at
a moment's notice
without having
to scramble.

GET READY TO HIT THE ROAD

WHEN DISASTER STRIKES, YOU DON'T HAVE TIME TO WASTE. ADVANCED PLANNING AND A PACKED-UP BAG ARE KEYS TO SUCCESS

You've got five minutes before the floodwaters or flames engulf your home and everything in it. What do you pack up and take with you? Called "go-bags" or "bug-out bags," these sacks of essential items are must-haves for any emergency. What you pack is up to you and not every bag fits every person. But here's the bottom line: You want to pack enough to survive, but not so much that you can't carry it all.

A bug-out bag isn't necessarily designed or intended to keep you alive indefinitely. The basic idea is to assemble a collection of gear and supplies that will sustain you until you reach your chosen location. Plan for the possibility that you'll be traveling on foot for some or all of your journey. If it turns out that you're able to ride in comfort and style the entire trip, all the better.

A good rule of thumb is to put away enough to survive for three days. Several companies offer ready-made go-bags, or you can stock one yourself. Choose a backpack with a solar panel, since electricity may be out. Here's what should go inside:

WATER

How much should you pack? Common sense says the hotter it is and the longer you have to trek, the more water you'll need. But it's the heaviest and bulkiest thing in the bag, so you can't go crazy. Most people can comfortably carry 2 liters of water, ideally divided between two containers so you can balance the load. You may also want to carry a water bottle with a filtration system. Never drink untreated or unfiltered water from a source you cannot absolutely trust. If you have at least one water container that is made of single-walled stainless steel, you can use it to boil water for disinfection, should the need arise.

FOOD

The focus should be on food items that can be eaten with little or no preparation. Think nonperishable, lightweight and portable, like individual peanut butter packs, meal replacement or protein bars, beef jerky and

FORM A FAMILY DISASTER PLAN

The Red Cross recommends this three-point strategy: Discuss potential emergencies, assign roles to each family member to work as a team, then practice the plan.

MAKE A ROSTER

Write down cell numbers and emails for everyone in your family; include other important phone numbers like school, work, neighbors where your kids spend time. Include names and descriptions of your pets, too. Make copies of the list for all family members.

HOW YOU'LL ESCAPE

List the kinds of disasters likely to strike, escape routes from the house and a meeting place if you get separated. Pick two places: one close to home and, in the event of a larger disaster, one farther away. Figure out alternative routes if the roads are blocked. And designate a couple of trusted people outside the family as contacts if you can't reach family members. If somebody has a disability or can't drive, work out a plan for them.

ASSIGN DUTIES

Figure out which family member will be in charge of assembling the go-bag. For disaster day, decide who will take the go-bag, who'll watch out for the pets and who'll monitor the radio for updates. Then assign someone the job of assembling everyone in the family every six months to go over the plan and update it as needed.

WATER WORKS Find nearby sources and purify as needed.

tuna in foil packs. Add some utensils and cookware, too. And don't forget your four-legged friends! If you're bugging out with your pet, be sure to bring some of his food along.

CLOTHING AND SHELTER

Pack enough clothing for a variety of temperatures and conditions, including rain and other storm conditions. That means water-resistant ponchos as well as several pairs of socks. The best blankets are those foil or mylar models that fold down to the size of a deck of cards. These will help you retain body heat and stay warm through the night. Add a small tarp and some cordage you can use for a quick tent or other shelter configuration. The idea is to get out from any rain, snow and wind that might cause you issues. You may also want to pack some big trash bags, which can turn into quick tents.

FIRE

Pack multiple fire-starters and different types of tinder so you are able to get a fire going quickly and easily should the need arise. Fire can disinfect water through boiling as well as cook food, keep you warm and light up a dark night. Practice using your fire-starters until you are confident you will be able to start a fire in all weather conditions.

FIRST-AID KITS

Most basic first-aid kits are just a start. Put away a few day's supply of your regular prescription medications, along with pain reliever like ibuprofen or acetaminophen. Add meds for stomach ailments such as diarrhea and indigestion, as well as cold remedies. Triple-antibiotic ointment will help reduce the possibility of infection from cuts and scrapes. Throw in a few surgical or respirator masks; many disasters can make breathing conditions harsh. Having the means to keep at least somewhat clean will help reduce the risks of infection and illness, too. A bar of soap and a washcloth can be used for quick clean-ups. Use hand sanitizer after bathroom breaks. Bath wipes are great—and don't forget toilet paper.

MULTIPURPOSE TOOLS

A multitool, like a Swiss Army knife, is a must. This gadget is like a "tool box for your pocket." A compass, a solar flashlight (or a high-quality flashlight and an extra set of batteries) and a hand-cranked emergency radio (so you'll be up-to-date on conditions, evacuations and shelter locations) should also be included. Duct tape is always useful. Wrap it on a pencil to save space and weight. Cordage is another must-have. Add an extra cellphone and charger—cell towers will be among the first things fixed in a disaster.

COPIES OF VITAL DOCUMENTS

The U.S. State Department, whose embassy officials have had to pack up in a hurry, suggests including copies of birth certificates, stock certificates and property deeds (put the originals in a safe-deposit box). Remember your insurance papers, too. It'll be difficult to file a flood insurance claim if the policy is stuck under water. Pack copies of banking and 401(k) statements, driver's licenses, Social Security cards and passports, too. And bring at least $50 to $100 in cash. ATMs will be down, as may debit/credit card readers, and banks may not open for days.

RADIO AHEAD
Don't just rely on
your phone for
communications—
service may go out.

STAYING IN TOUCH

Having some backup options in place will keep your whole family safer

When an emergency happens, one of the first things you'll want to do is find out if your loved ones are safe. Unless they are within arm's reach, you'll need a communication tool to connect. In addition, communication tools allow you to gather information about the situation. And that helps you make intelligent decisions about how to proceed, rather than having to rely on gut feelings and guesswork. Fortunately, we live in a time when we have many options, both high- and low-tech, to choose from.

CELLPHONES

While cellphones are the typical "go-to" for getting in touch with someone, you can't always count on them. In a major disaster, one of the first things to disappear is reliable cell service. The systems quickly become overloaded because everyone has the same thought: "I need to make sure my kids are OK!" Voice calls often won't go through. Text messages, because they use a slightly different system, might still be worth a shot—but there are no guarantees.

SMARTPHONE APPS

If you're able to connect to the internet, there are many different options for instant message programs and applications. Remember that anyone with whom you want to communicate will need to have the same app installed and running.

• Facebook Messenger operates independently of the Facebook app, meaning that while you do need a Facebook account to use it, Messenger can be opened and operated without going through the Facebook website or app. Like all technology, it isn't infallible—but when it works, it works well.

• Zello came into prominence in the aftermath of Hurricane Harvey. It allows you to use a cellphone like a walkie-talkie. Rather than placing calls, you're connecting with anyone who is listening on the channel you select. You can also connect with someone privately rather than over the open air. However, Zello does require an Internet connection in order to operate.

SOCIAL MEDIA

Even if you neither have nor want Facebook Messenger, you can still use social media to keep in touch. In fact, it has become commonplace in the wake of major disasters for people to create relevant groups on Facebook. For example, let's say you live in Anytown, USA, and there is a major flood. A group called something like Anytown Flood 2020 will be created on Facebook. You can join the group and immediately communicate with people to look for assistance, lend support and share information. Social media can be used to connect with rescuers, request help or just to mark yourself safe so friends and family know you're OK.

TWO-WAY RADIOS

Many families have invested in small two-way radios for use when attending events like county fairs, festivals and ski trips. But be wary of relying on these for anything beyond casual communication. Despite what the package might indicate, the range on these radios is minimal and is greatly affected by buildings, trees and other obstacles. Further, anyone with a radio tuned to the same channel can hear everything being said.

EMERGENCY RADIOS

These come in different styles and with various features. Look for one that will tune in to AM/FM as well as National Oceanic and Atmospheric Administration (NOAA) broadcasts, at a minimum. If you can afford the step-up, look for one that will also allow you to listen to shortwave (SW) broadcasts. Most of these radios will operate using batteries, dynamo or crank power. Some add a small solar panel as well. Many of them will charge a cellphone or other device via USB. While these radios don't allow for two-way communication, they will allow you to gather information.

STAY CALM
In a crisis,
panicking will
only get you into
more trouble.

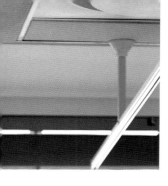

THE WILL TO LIVE

WHEN THE GOING GETS TOUGH, LEARN HOW TO CONQUER YOUR NEGATIVE EMOTIONS AND THOUGHTS AND TAKE PRACTICAL STEPS TO GET THROUGH

> The most important survival tool you possess lies between your ears. No matter what discouraging situation you find yourself in, from fleeing a wildfire to coming face-to-face with a mugger, your mind is powerful enough to help you through the crisis. On the other hand, if you focus on negative thoughts, your mind can convince you that you aren't going to make it. Here's how to stay mentally tough.

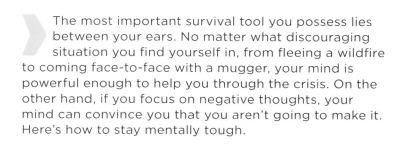

POSITIVE THINKING

Your attitude is crucial because the body will follow the mind. Repeat something to yourself enough times and your brain will make it happen. Sadly, the reverse is true: If you tell yourself that you can't do something or face a fear, you're dead in the water.

A study by researchers from the Cedars-Sinai Department of Psychiatry and Department of Medicine found that one in three medical patients shows symptoms of depression, and that depression could delay patients' recovery times, increase the length of hospital stays and increase the frequency of readmissions. Often, the more negative a patient thinks, the less likely he or she will be to take keep up with medical care.

If the odds seem like they're against you, don't panic! This is the time to concentrate on the power of positive thinking. If you find yourself getting overwhelmed and scared, repeat to yourself that things will get better and that you've overcome worse situations. If you're facing an illness, follow doctors' orders and take any medications they prescribe. Feeling better physically will help you feel better mentally, and vice versa.

HARNESS YOUR ANGER

For some people, anger can be a great motivator if it's kept under control. Some studies have even shown that anger actually helps people to think more rationally. But it's imperative that you use the emotion for good and not let it use you. If you let anger run the show, you run the risk of making snap decisions that may not be in your favor.

A good way to instantly calm yourself and quell your anger is to focus on your breathing: Breathe in through your nose and out through your mouth. Try everything you can to refocus your negative, angry thoughts to more positive ones.

STRENGTHEN YOUR WILL

Strength of will is a single-minded determination that you will overcome any hardship you're battling. While this ties in with positive thinking, this is a more base-level response. Think of positive thinking as being your own cheerleader, whereas strength of will is athletic ability that allows you to compete (and win!) when you're out there on the field. You must believe, at a molecular level, that nothing can stop you.

TOOLS FOR A SURVIVAL MINDSET

One of the greatest ways to foster a survival mindset in a truly awful situation is to find the motivation to recover. For some people, that can be difficult. What helps is to keep an item or two with you that will not only bring psychological comfort but provide motivation to survive, even thrive, and return home to your family and friends as soon as that's possible. Perhaps a photo or two of your loved ones will give you something to concentrate on as you wait in the doctor's office or spend some challenging nights alone in the hospital. Another option might be a pocket-size version of the religious text of your preference. Prayer goes hand in hand with positive thinking. Anything that will motivate you to prevail is welcome. Use whatever it takes.

ADAPTABILITY

One of the most important subsets of the mindset of a survivor is being able to adapt to changes in their situation. Many times we focus on a single track or plan, and when it doesn't pan out, we literally stop in our tracks because we don't know what to do. Think of it like going on a road trip. You've planned out the route and driving along when suddenly there's a detour sign. Now what? It can be easy to make that decision when you're just out for a leisurely drive. Worst case scenario, you end up seeing part of the town or countryside you've never visited before. But if this happens when you're running late for a job interview, that pressure means suddenly making decisions can be much more difficult. Go a step further and instead of being late to an interview, you're facing what feels like life or death. Once you make a plan, you might be terrified to deviate from it the least little bit, in case doing so might lead to a very negative outcome.

We need to be able to roll with the changes or adjust plans to fit. In a true survival situation, any plan of action needs to be fluid. There are inevitably going to be things that come up that were unexpected. Getting upset and stressed-out because a plan didn't work is just a waste of energy that you can't afford.

FIGHT OR FLIGHT

Our bodies and minds prepare to either dive into combat or run like hell away from it. Our brains are wired for deep thinking when we have time for it, but when the chips are down we often default to snap decisions, sometimes taking action without even realizing we decided to do so.

In some cases, that's the desired response. We practice and drill so that we can react to danger and threats without having to think it through. If you're attacked by a mugger, the last thing you want is for your brain to seize up and muddle through different options. Instead, you want to take decisive action and remove yourself from danger as quickly as possible.

Fortunately, there are ways we can teach our brains to react more sensibly and effectively in these situations. Learn how to use the fight-or-flight response in a positive manner, rather than as just an adrenaline dump that makes you shiver and feel nauseous. For a potentially dangerous physical threat (like encountering a mugger), you can invest in serious study in a practical martial art. Just knowing what to expect when you face danger can go a long way toward helping you to control your mind's reaction. Remember: The mind decides what the body will do.

BEST FRIENDS
Your pets are
counting on you
to keep them
comfortable in
emergencies.

SOS 101

Don't plan on
feeding pets people
food—it can upset
their digestion.

KEEPING PETS SAFE

PLAN AHEAD FOR YOUR FOUR-LEGGED FAMILY MEMBERS

> For many, pets are just as much a part of the family as any member who walks on two legs. We would no sooner leave a dog or cat to fend for itself after a disaster than we would a child. Even so, as we go about planning for emergencies, we sometimes overlook the needs of our furry friends.

Our critters rely upon us to provide their food, water and other necessities. Many breeds of dogs wouldn't be able to survive for very long on their own simply because they are unable to hunt very well. Selective breeding over the years has led to some types of dogs having short legs and little to no snout. These, among other genetic modifications, would make survival on their own difficult. Odds are high that they would just end up as dinner for something else.

Although we know that pets come in many varieties, we'll focus on dogs and cats here—the two popular pet choices in the United States. The recommendations provided, though, are applicable across the board. Just tweak them to suit your animal's individual needs.

WATER

Water is as important to animals as it is to humans. It is critical to account for the hydration needs of all of your pets as you calculate the water needs of the entire family or household. However, it is difficult, if not impossible, to recommend a specific amount of water to be stored for each animal, given the vast size differences out there. A German shepherd is going to require more water on a daily basis than, say, a Chihuahua.

One easy approach is to keep track of how much water your pets go through each day for three or four days and calculate an average. Multiply that by the number of days you feel you may end up on your own after a disaster and you'll know how much water to store. Tack on an additional 10 percent as a cushion, just in case.

FOOD

There is a school of thought out there that says pet owners can just feed their animals "people food" during a disaster. There is a whole lot wrong with that line of thinking. Think back to the last time Fido got into the garbage. Odds are the digestive upset that followed wasn't pleasant. By feeding him portions of your own rations, you're not only reducing the number of calories available for yourself and the other human family members, but you're possibly depriving man's best friend of the nutrients he truly needs.

Just like people, animals can get upset stomachs from a rapid change in diet. Your best bet is to stick with their normal food for as long as possible. As with water, determine how much food you'll need to store by figuring a per day–average consumption and multiplying that by the number of days you want to cover.

DON'T LEAVE YOUR PETS TIED UP!

Many pet owners have tie-outs set up in the yard so their dogs can be left out to do their business. In the wakes of Hurricanes Harvey and Irma, many people evacuated and, for logic known only to themselves, left their dogs tied out when they headed out of town. As the areas flooded, those animals met tragic ends. If you need to evacuate and for some reason you aren't able to take your animals with you, don't leave them trapped! Untie them and at least give them a chance.

HAVE A BACKUP
Make arrangements with neighbors to check in on your animals if you can't.

If you're storing dry food, one great option is to use a 5-gallon pail and a Gamma lid. The pail can be sourced from a local restaurant, deli or bakery. Often, these businesses have at least a few that used to contain pickles, frosting or some other food item. Wash them out, rinse well, and let them air-dry completely before filling. A Gamma lid is a gadget that attaches to the top of the pail and provides an airtight screw-on lid. These are far easier to open than the snap-on lids that are usually used to seal these pails. Gamma lids can be found at several places online as well as at many home-improvement stores.

As you buy new bags of food, rotate the emergency supply so you always have the freshest food possible stored. Canned food should be used up and replenished regularly. Always use the oldest cans first. If your pet typically only eats half a can and you usually store the other half in the refrigerator, remember that if the power is out, keeping the food cool might be difficult. If you can't buy smaller cans, you may end up having to throw away part of a can each day so you don't risk spoilage. Adjust your storage accordingly.

Make sure you have a couple of manual can openers stashed somewhere in the house. While many canned goods are equipped with pull tabs these days, Murphy's Law says at least one or two of them are sure to just snap off when you don't have any other way of opening the cans.

SANITATION

In an ideal world, any animals that would normally do their business outside will be able to do so during a time of crisis. The reality: There are any number of emergencies that would cause you to decide that allowing your pups and/or kitties to go out to the backyard is a bad idea.

One option is to pick up a kiddie pool when they go on clearance at the end of the summer. Should the need arise, the pool can be put on the floor in the basement or perhaps in a bedroom that will otherwise be kept unused for the duration of the emergency. Line the bottom with newspapers and dispose of the waste in garbage bags.

Any hard-surface floor will suffice, but the pool or something similar will help keep things contained.

COVER everlite/Getty Images **2-3** Romolo Tavani/Shutterstock **4-5** From left: Alamy; E+/Getty Images; Simon Fuller Imagery/Getty Images; Ken Kiefer 2/Getty Images; Per-Anders Pettersson/Getty Images; Thiago B Trevisan/Shutterstock; ninjaMonkeyStudio/Getty Images; iStockphoto/Getty Images **6-7** Colin Anderson/Getty Images **8-9** E+/Getty Images **10** NOAA/AP Photo; Mario Tama/Getty Images **12** AFP/Getty Images **13** Chip Somodevilla/Getty Images **14** New York Daily News Archive/Getty Images **15** Melanie Stetson Freeman/Getty Images **16-17** NZP Chasers/Getty Images **18** Jason Kempin/Getty Images **19** Rusty Russell/Getty Images **20-23** Scott Olson/Getty Images (3) **24** Pichit Sansupa/Shutterstock **25** Marcus Yam/Los Angeles Times/Getty Images **26-27** Westend61/Getty Images **28-29** Phil Yeo/Getty Images **30-31** David Frey/Getty Images **32** AFP/Getty Images **33** Marcus Yam/Los Angeles Times/Getty Images **34-35** JIJI PRESS/Getty Images **36** MARTIN BERNETTI/Getty Images **37** Samuel Berthelot Photography/Getty Images **38-39** Haje Jan Kamps /Getty Images; AFP/Getty Images **41** Ryan Pierse/Getty Images **42-43** RafalBelzowski/Getty Images **44-45** Anadolu Agency/Getty Images **46-47** Kiichiro Sato/AP/Shutterstock **48** Alamy **50-51** John Sirlin /EyeEm/Getty Images **52** picture alliance/Getty Images **53** Helen H. Richardson/Getty Images **54-55** Simon Fuller Imagery/Getty Images **56** Santa Monica Police Department/Getty Images **58-59** Corbis/Getty Images; Jefferson County Sheriff's Department/Getty Images **60-61** Scott Olson/Getty Images; Jessica Hill/AP Photo **62** David Becker/Getty Images **64** Andrew Regam/Getty Images **66** Stocktrek Images/Getty Images **67** Justin Lane-Pool/Getty Images **68-69** Remi Benali/Getty Images **70** VALERY HACHE/Getty Images (2) **71** Igor Golovniov/SOPA Images/Shutterstock **72-73** South_agency/Getty Images **75** Zoran Kolundzija/Getty Images **76** boonchai wedmakawand/Getty Images **78-79** Witthaya Prasongsin /EyeEm/Getty Images **80-81** Clockwise from left: MAURICIO LIMA/Getty Images (2); DPA/Getty Images **82-83** Ken Kiefer 2/Getty Images **84-85** iStockphoto/Getty Images **87** Sports Studio Photos/Getty Images **88-89** Andres Ruggeri/EyeEm/Getty Images **90** EBENP/AP Photo; Rebecca S. Gratz/Getty Images **93** jhorrocks/Getty Images **94** Baranov E/Shutterstock **95** Anthony Saint James/Getty Images **96-97** nechaev-kon/Getty Images **98** Thierry FALISE/Gamma-Rapho/Getty Images **99** PM Images/Getty Images **100-101** Per-Anders Pettersson/Getty Images **102-103** Robert Shafer/Getty Images **104** DeepDesertPhoto/Getty Images **105** Franz Aberham/Getty Images **106-107** ROBERTO SCHMIDT/Getty Images **108** PHOTO 24/Getty Images **110-111** Justin Case/Getty Images **112** Reimar Gelke/EyeEm/Getty Images **113** Image Source/Getty Images **114** Richmatts/Getty Images **115** JAVIER CANTELLOPS/Getty Images **116-117** Thiago B Trevisan/Shutterstock **118-119** The Asahi Shimbun/Getty Images **120** Dave Chan/Getty Images **121** Peter Foley/EPA/Shutterstock **122** Bruce Asato/Getty Images **124-125** Rachel La Corte/Getty Images **126-127** MIGUEL MEDINA/Getty Images **128-129** stevecoleimages/Getty Images **130** Josh Coleman/Getty Images **131** Gabriel Diaz/Stocksy **132-133** Laura Lezza/Getty Images **134** Ralph White/Getty Images **135** asbe/Getty Images **136-137** ninjaMonkeyStudio/Getty Images **138-139** David Pereiras/EyeEm/Getty Images **141** picture alliance/Getty Images **143** dowell/Getty Images **145** Ali Majdfar/Getty Images **146-147** KREML/Shutterstocdk **148** Pallava Bagla/Getty Images **150-151** Malcolm Schuyl/Flpa/imageBROKER/Shutterstock **152-153** Alamy **154** Wojtek Laski/Getty Images **155** The Asahi Shimbun/Getty Images **156-157** Science Photo Library/Getty Images **158-159** iStockphoto/Getty Images **161** wavebreakmedia/Shutterstock **163** Alamy **164-165** Dovapi/Getty Images **167** wellphoto/Getty Images **168-169** ukmng/Shutterstock **170-171** Kwikee.com **172-173** schfer/Getty Images **175** Aleksandra Suzi/Shutterstock **176** Gal2007/Getty Images **178-179** Portra Images/Getty Images **181** Joe Raedle/Getty Images **182-183** Bryce Hughes/EyeEm/Getty Images **185** Elise Chehowski/EyeEm/Getty Images

SPECIAL THANKS TO CONTRIBUTING WRITERS:

JIM COBB, MIKE ROTHSCHILD, ASHLEIGH RUHL AND DAWN YANEK

CENTENNIAL BOOKS

An Imprint of
Centennial Media, LLC
40 Worth St., 10th Floor
New York, NY 10013, U.S.A.

ISBN 978-1-951274-29-0

Distributed by
Simon & Schuster, Inc.
1230 Avenue of the Americas
New York, NY 10020, U.S.A.

For information about custom editions, special sales and premium and corporate purchases,
please contact Centennial Media at contact@centennialmedia.com.

Manufactured in Malaysia

Publishers & Co-Founders Ben Harris, Sebastian Raatz
Editorial Director Annabel Vered
Creative Director Jessica Power
Executive Editor Janet Giovanelli
Deputy Editors Ron Kelly, Alyssa Shaffer
Design Director Ben Margherita
Art Directors Andrea Lukeman,
Natali Suasnavas, Joseph Ulatowski
Assistant Art Director Jaclyn Loney
Photo Editor Christina Creutz
Production Manager Paul Rodina
Production Assistant Alyssa Swiderski
Editorial Assistant Tiana Schippa

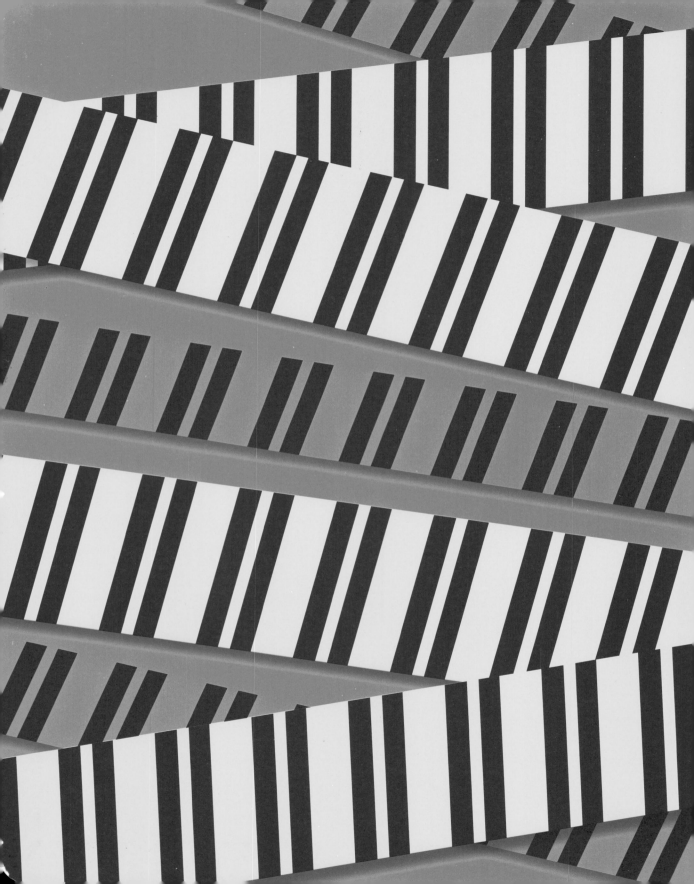